Business
is Personal

Business
is Personal

The Truth About What it
Takes to Be Successful While
Staying True to Yourself

BETHENNY
FRANKEL

AND KAREN KELLY

hachette
BOOKS

NEW YORK

Hachette Go, an imprint of Hachette Books

Hachette Book Group
1290 Avenue of the Americas
New York, NY 10104
HachetteGo.com
Facebook.com/HachetteGo
Instagram.com/HachetteGo

First Edition: May 2022

Hachette Books is a division of Hachette Book Group, Inc.

The Hachette Go and Hachette Books name and logos are trademarks of Hachette Book Group, Inc.

The publisher is not responsible for websites (or their content) that are not owned by the publisher.

Library of Congress Control Number: 2022930715

ISBNs: 978-0-306-82703-7 (hardcover), 978-0-306-82705-1 (ebook), 978-0-306-83117-1 (signed edition), 978-0-306-83116-4 (B&N.com signed edition)

Printed in the United States of America

LSC-C

Printing 1, 2022

This book is dedicated to strong women. We are the rock and the glue; beautiful on the inside and outside, and often just trying to hold it together. Motherhood is hard. Work is hard. Nothing good comes easy, so we work endlessly on our careers, families, homes, friendships, relationships, and sometimes, last but not least, on ourselves.

We are fierce. We muster strength when we really think we have no more to give. We try to do good in the world and in our personal lives while attempting to look decent, exercise, be intimate, get a good night's sleep, and find spiritual meaning in our lives.

I have learned about relationships, parenting, sex, miscarriages, philanthropy, politics, entertainment, family, and the right thing to do from women. We have been on this mission together and we have a good part of this crazy journey left.

I celebrate women and our ability to come from a place of yes, and simply keep going under any and all circumstances. We are the ultimate multitaskers.

Thank you for giving me the inspiration to write this book. I write for myself, for you, for my precious, beautiful daughter, and for all the wonderful women in the world.

XO – B

CONTENTS

INTRODUCTION

Dive In, Strive, Thrive, Repeat

WELCOME TO MY WORLD.

You're holding in your hands a business book, but it's not typical for the genre. It doesn't look back in reflection after a storied career has ended. I'm at a critical juncture and evolutionary moment in my working life, and I'm not done yet, not by a long shot. I'm an idea hamster, addicted to innovation. It's in my DNA. It's not always easy being a person who is constantly thinking, but it's the way I activate myself.

Business is Personal is about how I got to be where I am right now, which is a good and hard-earned place. However, the journey has not been without challenges. Even today, I continue to look for ways to work smarter, leaner, and more streamlined. I struggle with balance, a word you'll see a lot in this book. I can find myself in a constant battle with the weeds, and admittedly, I do sweat the small stuff. Many people define themselves by how crowded their calendars are, but that's not for me. I want to be unshackled so I can use my time wisely to create and give back in ways that are meaningful to me.

I'm the get-it-done, don't-complain-or-explain type, but I also think about existential questions like what is the meaning of life, and what path should I travel now that my fiftieth birthday is in the rearview mirror?

I've come far enough in my professional trajectory—I've written and published ten books (all on my smartphone); hit the cover of *Forbes* in 2011; and developed several successful product lines, cementing my credibility as a bona fide business person—to have valuable insights to offer about how to succeed as an entrepreneur and as an independent person in a crazy, unpredictable world. Many of my businesses were hits, but others weren't. Early in my career, my healthy baking business, BethennyBakes, had challenges getting off the ground. A company called Princess Pashmina, which sold affordably priced luxury shawls, was successful until it wasn't. I am also the founder and CEO of Skinnygirl, a global lifestyle empire, featuring products for women that offer practical and stylish solutions to everyday problems. My product portfolio includes several food and drink products including coffee, popcorn, and preserves; apparel; shapewear; supplements; and cookware. I have also created Bethenny, an elevated brand that includes products like sunglasses. My charitable organization, the B Strong Initiative, provides aid in the time of crisis in the United States and across the globe. I have learned many lessons from all of these efforts, and I've evolved from young, single, and broke to a mature businesswoman and philanthropist.

I truly believe that success is achievable for anyone who wants to put in old-school effort and hard work. *Business is Personal* gives you tools that are applicable to so many life situations, and as the title says, business *is* personal. Work, love, life: it's all intertwined.

By my sharing my mistakes and victories I hope you come away with a renewed feeling of pride for what you've done, and for what you can do to take advantage of your assets and talents. I use many examples in this book that come from my life as an entrepreneur, philanthropist, and businesswoman.

I don't want you to feel that because you have not achieved a certain level in your career or size in your business that these examples don't apply to you, because they do. I began where so many people start: from scratch, with nothing, and building a business brick by brick. I was in my late thirties and still could not afford a taxi in Manhattan. I would bounce checks and see "insufficient funds" notices at the ATM. I'm a late bloomer, so I know for a *fact* that you can start succeeding anytime. The tools and stories in this book will help you do this.

Business is Personal is also filled with insights from a wide variety of business moguls and game-changers whom I've had the privilege to talk to, including Facebook CEO Sheryl Sandberg; actor Matthew McConaughey; entrepreneur Mark Cuban; former senator and presidential candidate Hillary Clinton; journalist and novelist Candace Bushnell; tech journalist Kara Swisher; shoe designer Steve Madden; Panera Bread CEO Niren Chaudhary; finance expert and TV host Jim Cramer; actress, author, and entrepreneur Suzanne Somers, and others. Their advice and insights alone are worth the price of admission!

In the stories I share, I reveal what it takes to be successful in business while balancing the rest of your life. Whether it's spending time with my daughter; scheduling her day and our time together; planning a trip with my fiancé, Paul; or just making room for a personal recharge, balance requires deliberate thought. I'm a perfectionist to a fault, and I like a neat and tidy environment. I accept this aspect of myself and have built a life that supports it. Someone else might be super successful and work extremely hard but they probably have a junk drawer in their kitchen. I don't have a junk drawer in my kitchen, and I don't have a junk drawer in my business or life. Admittedly, it's hard to keep up with me, if I'm being totally transparent. But that's okay. It works for me. You must find what works for you.

Business is Personal is written in the voice you've come to know and trust: transparent, honest, sometimes profane, often funny, and never boring. I'm not modest about my accomplishments; I'm proud of them. When you're done reading, I want you to understand your own strengths and go out and use them.

A story is not worth telling unless you're going to lay it all out from top to bottom so people can learn from it. I share how the Skinnygirl sale to Beam happened, including what I considered when we were putting the deal together before I had even made one penny from the brand and didn't even know I had something to sell. I talk about how my podcast evolved from a small venture into a multi-million-dollar program; why I left *The Real Housewives of New York City* (and walked away from a lot of money); and how I solved serious product problems before they became major catastrophes.

My decisions and actions are strategic. I'm not saying they're a win every time. Mistakes get made, especially when you're just one person who can't keep her eye on every single ball. Having a great team is important too. However, the products I develop and the deals I make all have a method and plan behind them. It's frustrating because the press can sometimes present every success as if it happened overnight, like magic, without showing all of the time and energy behind it on my part. It can seem as if these successes happened *to* me instead of being orchestrated and led *by* me. The seeds I plant that no one but me sees *do* grow into trees and eventually into forests—people see a forest without considering that it started out as an empty field of soil. That's the kind of gardening I explain in this book, so that you understand how the growth happened. It's always been the result of care and feeding in the form of a series of granular, meticulous, detailed, intentional, and strategic decisions that I make every single day.

Trust me, everything that I've done was and is done with intention. As someone who sits in the bull's-eye of the demographic that I want my brands to reach, I have a personal and practical sense of what women want and need, and I put that knowledge to work every day, even on products that may not hit the shelf for several years. One chess move I make today could come to fruition five years from now, and it will have been worth the wait.

Why did I write *Business is Personal* now? I want to inspire you the way you've inspired me. So many of you have evolved with me over time; you've stayed on the ride since the beginning. I am so grateful to all of my fans who have supported me. Every day you make me want to be better than I was the day before. I also believe that it's a great time to start a business. The playing field has been leveled in so many ways. We have lived through a world-shifting event, a pandemic, during which many of us stayed home and had a chance to reevaluate why we were going into an office every day to collect a paycheck, and whether that was satisfying or not. Technology also makes a lot of things possible for entrepreneurs that didn't exist even ten years ago, like digital meetings, on-demand manufacturing capabilities, and fingertip access to more people and ideas.

In a world where the snow globe has been shaken, and everything is upside down, you can find tremendous opportunities. Economic uncertainty and financial downturn can be an ideal time to launch a new business, place bold bets, and build enduring brands.

Instead of panicking and jumping on the complaining or blaming bandwagon, I collect myself, assess the situation, and decide where I can be effective and productive. You have to think about difficult or unusual times and circumstances in this way—another philosophy you will find in this book.

You have to be honest with yourself. Not everybody is cut out for every kind of business. You can't exclusively rely on a good idea or a relentless work ethic to launch you out of the entrepreneurial starting gate—you need to learn strategic thinking. But for sure, you need to get on the goddamn road, pick a lane, and keep moving forward, past and around roadblocks, detours, and bad weather. You may get a flat tire or run out of gas, but you have to get back in the car, which will take you to another road. Don't stay stuck and stunted in some fictitious dead end, one-way street business plan that you may never finish or even start.

Remember, nobody, not even the so-called experts, knows what the hell they're doing all the time. No one has all the answers, not me, not anyone. That means you need to raise your personal antennae. If something feels wrong, it's wrong; if something feels right, it's right. Even if you're wrong you can fix it, and solving problems becomes part of learning and making better, more informed decisions the next time. I always want to be in solution mode. Of course, you can and should ask other people for their opinions. Most of the time, I am decisive and know what to do and what not to do.

Sometimes, especially if I am venturing into an area that is new to me, I like to crowdsource or ask questions of experts and those with unique experience in certain fields. I take everything into consideration, and then I go with my gut. Experts are often used to doing things in a certain way. Many are geniuses and quite brilliant, but some don't like to go outside of what works for them.

But that may not work for me, and it may not work for you. Listen and learn, but make your own decisions. Build your own success tool kit by cherry-picking from all the good advice you find or receive, including what you find in this book. It's why I wrote this book, and why I developed my podcast, *Just B*—to share advice from successful people who represent all walks of life, upbringing, backgrounds, and so on.

The ability to discern between good deals and bad ones, honest people and those who are less than transparent, is based on understanding, seeing the big picture, looking at the details, and asking questions—but a lot of it comes from your gut, from pulling back and thinking. Ask questions, seek answers, reach out, but at the end of the day, figure out what is right for you. Create your own road map.

The same qualities people used in the 1950s to become successful are the same traits you need today: confidence, drive, passion, persistence, and stick-to-itiveness. Despite what it may seem, no one TikTok dances themselves into genuine, sustainable success. You can think that it is working, but it's fool's gold. The truth is, you have to be willing to get past the finish line and then go the extra mile, figure out solutions to dilemmas, and solve your own problems from what I call a place of yes. Starting from no is a dead-end proposition.

The Skinnygirl cocktail is celebrated today because it succeeded by creating a new category, and the first for a woman in the industry. Every restaurant or bar you go into has a "skinny" cocktail or some version of it, and that is entirely because of me. Every skinny latte, syrup, and pizza are because of that one idea I had for a low-calorie but delicious margarita. But it almost didn't succeed. My original partner wouldn't spend money ahead of the brand. We couldn't keep up with demand, even though a consumer should be able to buy a thirteen-dollar product easily. We faced everything from a glass shortage to an agave shortage. It was a nightmare. More on that later; my point is you push through it. If you keep hitting a wall, you step back and you just find another way through. Saying yes means continuing to come at problems in different ways, and stop doing what's not working.

The thirteen chapters in this book are based around what some of my team members call "Bethenny-isms"—the tools I use when it comes to making good choices, building a brand, staying five steps ahead of the game, and maintaining my sanity in a fast-paced and always changing business environment. B SMART boxes in each chapter highlight tips and insights you can apply today, right now, in your own efforts at continual improvement. The case studies I share are from my real-life dealings as I continue to build my brands, services, and products. Some of the stories I tell are yet to have an ending, so stay tuned!

If you make an investment of time and money in this book, I want you to get value from it. That could be a new perspective on your own business, or inspiration to try something new, take a risk, and live to your full potential. I'm not the touchy-feely type, but it would give me a feeling of satisfaction to know that I helped you spread your wings. What matters are your attitude, your passion, your drive, your determination, and your willingness to work hard. These qualities are alive in this book, and they are the message I most want you to come away with. That's what I want *Business is Personal* to inspire in you. If you know you've got what it takes, don't spare anything—just go get what's yours.

1

You've Got to Be in It to Win It

THE BEGINNING OF ANYTHING IS THE HARDEST PART OF STARTING anything new. Where do I begin *Business is Personal*? In the same way I start anything: by going in feet first. Nike said it best: just do it. Get in the game.

I have heard more than my fair share of business advice and tips over the years, from small-business people, fellow entrepreneurs, and seasoned CEOs. But there is one piece of advice that a few people have offered that I reject. That is the idea that you need a perfect, well-thought-out business plan to begin working on an idea. It's not true. If you wait for a perfect plan, you never begin. You can often end up procrastinating and getting stuck. The perfectly organized closet might exist, the perfect beach might be out there in the Caribbean somewhere. But the perfect business plan? It doesn't exist. Most of the ideas and plans you write down won't happen anyway. Besides, when you make a plan, fate laughs. How about instead of planning, just get in the car, get on the road, and start driving, mapping your route as you go. Here's a piece of advice that has never let me down: you have to be in it to win it.

I talked to journalist and creator of the iconic *Sex and the City* franchise Candace Bushnell for my podcast, *Just B,* about the idea of starting from where you are. While her personal and professional stories are different from mine in many respects, they are also similar in some relevant ways, especially when it comes to full participation in these things we call life and work. Like me, she left home as a young woman. At nineteen years old, she ran away from her Texas college and moved to New York City to pursue her passion: writing. After selling a children's book to Simon & Schuster for a thousand dollars (it was never published), she juggled waitressing work with freelance writing gigs. She wanted to be a writer, which meant writing. It didn't necessarily mean going to college. Why wait?

Like me, she struggled for several years just to make ends meet. One job led to another, and just as I did, Candace built her professional network one person and one job at a time. Then, in 1993, she landed a gig writing for the *New York Observer.* There, she started a column about the single life in Manhattan that eventually became the mega-hit television and movie series *Sex and the City.* Candace's novels have all achieved bestseller status. Her success as a writer is cemented.

It didn't happen overnight. Candace was in it to win it. She was committed, tenacious, and always upping her game, honing her craft, looking for the next opportunity.

"I am successful because I worked hard, but you have to love doing it. I wrote for a long time without making any money. I still write a lot of stuff I do not get paid for and even today I think about whether I have enough money to write for the next two or five years. Sometimes you are riding on the wave and it works, but

the wave can change direction, and then you are not su_
she says. But you can't let that stop you. Like all successful people, Candace didn't quit when writing didn't pay off immediately. She did the work, and she kept at it because she loved it and had a passion for the writing world.

I didn't dream of being a writer when I was a little girl, nor did I imagine that I would become a food, beverage, and fashion mogul. However, I relate to Candace's early decision to go out on her own. We both knew we wanted to create something and be the captains of our own ships.

Develop an Independent Mindset

Every successful entrepreneur or self-made person comes to the realization at some point in their careers that success is up to them. Even as a child, I knew that if I was going to make it on my own, I had to be the main participant in my own destiny. No one was going to step in on my behalf. It was me or no one. For me, it was a logical and necessary assumption, because I didn't have a strong emotional family life. This was a motivating factor for me that had nothing to do with money. We weren't poor in a financial sense, but there was a poverty of normalcy in my house, a lack of stability. This was obvious to me when I looked at friends whom I knew *were* financially poor, but they had the wealth of strong emotional family safety nets. In that way, they were far richer than I. The good news is, everyone has struggles, and no one's life is perfect.

When some people are broke, fall on hard times, or hit a glitch in their personal or professional lives, they can be secure in the knowledge that family is there for them. That was not the case for me when I was growing up or as I strived to make a career for myself as a young woman in Manhattan. When I was in high school I remember having a high fever and a bubble on my belly. I didn't know what was wrong, so I called my friend Alyssa, because my mom was not available. Alyssa's mother took me to the hospital, and I was so grateful for that. It was chicken pox. Even though I recovered, the pain of not having my family there to comfort me was embarrassing. The chicken pox went away, but not having my family there was an emotional wound that never quite healed.

A similar scenario took place when I was a young woman living in the city. I was sick with pneumonia. I remember dragging myself to the corner bodega to buy some medicine, and I actually fainted right there in the store. The guy behind the deli counter picked me up off the floor and made sure I got home. I was visiting Florida once, and I became extremely ill with food poisoning. I remember crawling through the lobby of the St. Regis Hotel by myself to get to an urgent care facility. My friend at the time was able to meet me at urgent care, and that was reassuring, but it's not the same as having your mother take care of you. In Aspen, I almost died of anaphylactic shock, and another friend helped me, which not only saved my life, it also made me feel loved and taken care of. I absolutely have a network of friends who are there for me. What was missing was the powerful emotional safety net that a strong family unit provides.

Some people can move back in with mom and dad if they have to, or at a minimum, crash on their aunt or sister's couch until they get their shit together. That provides a cushion. That was never a possibility for me. I don't begrudge people who have those kinds of families at all—how fortunate! I just wasn't one of those people. No one was standing there ready to hand me a parachute if I started to free fall. The practice of being proactive has been extremely helpful to me as I developed as an entrepreneur. As Beyoncé said, shoes on my feet, I bought them—I depend on me. I always knew that if I ran into trouble, I might have to sleep in my crappy car with the broken windshield. It never happened, thankfully, but the possibility was always in the background.

When you're in that kind of life situation, it becomes clear much faster than it might for people who have stronger emotional backup that in order to be something, do something, or create something you cannot stand on the sidelines and wait for someone to come along and save you. You have to help yourself. This is especially true when it comes to making a living. I've never wanted to be shackled or tied down in any way. My pursuit of entrepreneurial interests and financial stability is a search for autonomy; freedom and autonomy. That's my main motivating factor.

I relate to Candace Bushnell in her realization that she had no option other than to make a life for herself. Her father, Calvin, who was a genius and one of the inventors of the air-cooled, hydrogen-air fuel cell that was used in the Apollo space missions in the 1960s, was also a strict pragmatist when it came to his three daughters. "There was pressure to do something with our lives, but no instructions on how to do it, or the offer of any help," she says. "He always told me that when I turned eighteen I'd be cut off." She took quite seriously the message that her family was not going to bankroll her once she became an adult, which is why she ditched college for New York and started doing what she wanted to do without waiting for permission.

It's not necessary to be in a situation that forces you to fend for yourself to develop an independent mindset. You can develop the fierceness and passion and drive to succeed by finding what you're passionate about, and making a commitment to doing whatever it takes to pursue that passion. You have to trust and believe that you and you alone are driving the car, because at the end of the day, you are.

Do the Work

If I am going to attempt something, if I am going to be *in* something—a job, a relationship, product development, motherhood—I have to make my best effort, or it is not worth doing. Good enough isn't good enough. Either do it well or don't do it at all. Failure was and always is a possibility, but at least I know that I gave it my best shot and participated fully, that I can rest easy knowing I gave it my best effort no matter what happens. Winning is much more of an option under those circumstances.

Billionaire entrepreneur, television personality, and media innovator Mark Cuban actually used the expression *do the work* when I talked to him about what success means. He told me, "People ask me, Mark, what business should I start? And I say, if you don't know, I can't tell you. But what I can tell you is that you have to do the work. You have to learn. One of the greatest assets you have is excitement about learning. It is the only constant in this life. Especially with all the changes we're going through right now. There are new things to come and you can't be ignorant to it. If you want to be successful you have to put in the time to learn."

While he conceded that the pandemic has been a terrible time in many ways—unemployment numbers grew high and many people felt upside down in their lives—we agreed there have also been opportunities. If you happen to have an online education program that you were working on, you were crushing it during the shutdown. If you happen to own commercial real estate, you were fucked. Despite uncertainty, there's always an opportunity for an individual to do the work and learn about how they can thrive in a unique circumstance. "Typically, when you start a company you're competing with a bunch of big companies that have a huge advantage financially, in experience, and in an existing customer base," Mark said. "Because of COVID, and everything that's happened, large companies were trying to figure out how to stay in business and deal with the social change. But if you are small and started from scratch you don't have those legacy problems. It's fascinating. The big companies are like cruise ships trying to move; they're just trying to stay on the water. Small companies and start-ups are nimble. They are sports cars; they can reverse course more easily. They don't have capital, they don't have anything, but they do have piss and vinegar and hard work. They can start small and just take off," he said.

We talked about looking back at 2020–2021 twenty years forward, and seeing the companies and entrepreneurs that were created during that time who succeeded because they did the work and had a vision for the future. "We're going to look back and see that the business reset in 2020 resulted in people saying 'I have a better idea, now let's go and work,'" he said.

I think that's true, but sometimes being ahead of the curve can be challenging. It can be hard to make people understand the benefits of something outside their comfort zone. In 2003, I started BethennyBakes, a natural and healthy baked goods business in New York, before wheat-, fat-, and dairy-free foods became as ubiquitous as they are today. It was way ahead of its time. People were not as attuned to this concept as they are now. Still, I persevered. I found a way to sell and distribute my goodies, and I built a small but loyal following. When I appeared as a contestant on *The Apprentice: Martha Stewart*, in 2005, there was nothing legal I wouldn't have done to win that show, because I believed that it could be the important first step in helping build BethennyBakes into a bigger, widely recognized company. More on that later—but

I feel like some of the determination displayed by so many successful people, myself included, is missing in people today. Why show up if you're not going to participate at your highest level?

Don't be the person who wants a promotion or a raise just for showing up. That's entitlement. No one is giving you anything; go get it. Earn the elevation by working harder and smarter than everyone else. It doesn't matter what level you're at: if you are working to succeed you can't rest on your laurels. I see how the approach to work plays out in some of the assistants I've had. I have had competent, excellent people working for me, and they're writing their own tickets through hard work. However, some of the assistants I've hired didn't want to work on weekends, or if they did, they wanted to know about overtime pay. They hadn't wanted to work past five or six o'clock; they didn't want to do any heavy lifting in terms of the effort it takes to execute a job—any job—at a high level.

Today I have a strong team, which I have worked diligently to curate, like an art collection. One of my assistants in particular will be a success as she moves through her career, because her work ethic is so strong. She will say to me, *I want you to feel supported, I will travel with you. What else can I do? How can I make this easier?* That means everything to me. Because she approaches the job with such vigor, loyalty, and enthusiasm, I'm careful about not letting her burn herself out. But I also see a lot of me in her, and I know that if she sustains this attitude toward work, she will be a success as she goes forward.

If people are inspired by me and what I've accomplished, that's thrilling. It's icing on the cake—I am not in the game, in business, to prove anything other than that I can create quality products that solve problems and inspire others. I want to be the best I can be and a success, because I don't want to waste my time on being anything less. If you can show enthusiasm and willingness to work hard, you immediately differentiate yourself from the competition. When Candace Bushnell landed an entry-level job at *Ladies' Home Journal*, she explained that "the first thing I had to do every morning was sharpen pencils and my boss said I was the best pencil sharpener that they had ever had!" I think that's great—if you are going to do something, no matter how trivial it seems, do the best you possibly can. It will pay off. It will get you noticed. That's what you should focus on!

People today often don't seem to have the same hunger to be the best pencil sharpener. We need to get that ambition back. In a world where everybody receives a medal for showing up, or complains about the fact that their identity holds them back, you can be a standout by showing up and working harder and smarter than everyone else. The bottom line is, there are no shortcuts if you want to succeed. There is no trick to being successful; it's hard work. That's rather comforting, because it means you don't have to come from a certain background, you just have to do the work and forget about everything else.

Let Your Work Speak for You

I never thought about being a woman in a man's world until a reporter asked me a question about it. People ask me about being a woman in a man's world, or what it's like to be a female entrepreneur. I don't look at the world that way. I think about being strong and pushing through. Maybe it's because I was brought up at the racetrack, maybe I was just born tough, I don't know. Coming in second by a nose doesn't count (which is interesting, because I came in second by a nose on *The Apprentice*). For instance, had

I thought about the fact that I was a woman in a business that is dominated by men, where men are the power behind and in front of the brands, maybe I wouldn't have gone into the spirits industry with my Skinnygirl margarita. It never occurred to me that some doors might be closed to me because I'm female.

Whatever I've wanted to do, I have just gone in and fought to do it. I've fought to be better than the men, better than the women, to just *be better than*. I am not interested in terms like "girlboss" and "bad bitch" because I am not in it to win it as a symbol for women or to prove something about my personality or identity. They're turnoffs and just not me. I have entered into more than one male-driven business and pushed through—the spirits business; even media has been largely male-dominated. I do female empowerment by showing it, not talking about it. I get that there is inequity. Gordon Gekko is a thing of the 1980s and Miranda Priestly is a thing of the 2000s. Anna Wintour is the biggest Head Bitch in Charge, or HBIC, the world has ever seen. She knows how to work eighteen hours a day without asking about her lunch break. That's how you get in to win. So many women exemplify this same philosophy—they don't screw around. If you want to get something done, ask a busy woman to do it.

When I am doing something, I am focused on the task at hand. I'm not self-conscious. I believe that is the best way to reach goals. Thinking of yourself in terms of your identity can hold you back. It can lead you to make assumptions about what other people may be thinking about you, like "he doesn't want to work with me because I'm a woman"—but it's generally not the case. Even if it is the case, focusing on that is not going to be helpful to you or your aspirations. That thinking is coming from a place of no, rather than from a place of yes. You can find a way around the naysayers by finding a way to do what you want to do and then being good at what you're doing. Jumping on an identity bandwagon that talks about "all men are garbage," or they have more privileges than women, or they always make more money and hold more power, or whatever, is not helpful, and it's also not always true. If you're in it to win it (and again, why bother if you're not?), any kind of thinking that puts you in a negative or defensive space pulls you down.

I could have allowed preconceived notions about women in the spirits industry to hold me back from entering the business, which is dominated by men. I didn't even think about what the industry would think of me because I was a woman. That said, spirits is the most competitive business ever. It's run by men, it's marketed to men, so you have to have a strong personality in order to deal with men and get your ideas through. You can't worry about sexism or barriers to women—you just have to go in and meet people where they are standing. By doing that, I changed the industry.

I had a fresh idea, one that no one had had before, when I created the Skinnygirl margarita, and that helped me get through what is a very competitive market. I cracked the code with a product that would appeal to women. Every liquor store is crowded with every idea. You can't get caught up in worries around what people will think of you. I basically pushed my idea through like I've never seen anybody else do, and turned the drink into a recognizable brand in less than two years, and then sold the business for millions of dollars in that short period of time.

My big-picture philosophy for being in it to win it is don't get caught up in "no" thinking—that's exactly what you're doing if you think you can't be in the game because you are too this or not enough that. Forget it! You're you, and you have to work on making yourself better every single day. Look for the yes.

> Don't get caught up in "no" thinking. Look for the yes.

Make the Call

Understanding you're on your own in your efforts doesn't mean you can do it all alone. I'm not contradicting myself here. I've never been shy about finding experts, asking questions, and getting my ideas to the right people. In it to win it is being proactive. Introduce yourself. Pick up the phone. Write the email. Today, there may be people who come to me wanting to partner. But many times, I still make the effort to reach out to them. No one is too small to introduce themselves to someone in a position to help or advise . . . or too big to stop trying. Be willing to ask questions and seek knowledge. I've called Gary Janetti, a writer from the television show *Family Guy,* and Food Network's Bobby Flay to ask a question. There are so many others I've called, and I'm always surprised at how gracious people are with their time—if you don't waste theirs.

So now you might be thinking, *But I'm a nobody. No one will take my call. I don't know anyone powerful and I have no clout.* Good news: So what? None of that matters. I made calls when I was a nobody, and I got through to people because I was smart and prepared. People are much more accessible than you imagine them to be. I will cold call anyone, and you would be surprised how many people will take my call. Yes, I understand that at this point in my career more people will take my calls than perhaps they would have in the past. You might be surprised at how many people would call me back when I made the effort to connect, yes, even when Bethenny Frankel was not a recognized name. You have to be brave. Courage is a big part of being in it to win it.

It's easier than you think to reach influential people. Years ago, when I was working on my BethennyBakes business, I would watch Food Network shows and wait for the credits to roll at the end of the show. I'd take down the names of production companies and producers, then I'd call information and get the phone numbers of those companies, and call and ask for email addresses of the producers. Generally the receptionist would be more than happy to provide the right contact information. I'd bake cookies, pack them up, and send them to the producers and executives at their offices along with a personal handwritten note. I'd follow up with a phone call, and oftentimes, I'd get a meeting with them. It didn't result in a cooking show, but I was building contacts, connecting with people, and becoming known. It was groundwork.

I was a hostess at the Los Angeles restaurant La Scala, where the chopped salad was invented. There I met and connected with many different people, which is how I became an assistant for Kathy Hilton, entrepreneur, philanthropist, and mother to Paris and Nicky Hilton, and film and television producer Jerry Bruckheimer. I introduced myself, exchanged contact information, and made myself available to these people when they needed an assistant. At a bar in New York called JG Melon, I met a man who helped me get a job as the actor, writer, and comedian Denis Leary's chef when he was doing his acclaimed television series *Rescue Me*. That was an interesting job—I cooked in a trailer every day for all the actor firefighters on the set. The bottom line is, I made all of these things happen *before* I appeared on *The Real Housewives of New York City*, *before* anyone knew who I was, because I was proactive about talking to people, not because I wanted to **Make business personal.** make friends or have an exciting social life (I'm a homebody), but because I wanted to develop and grow as an independent person and entrepreneur.

At its inception, my goal for the *Just B* podcast was to express myself and to have unique conversations with important people who could help listeners create their own tool boxes for success in their own ways. I focused on people who had done something to change their field or industry, who were breakthrough business people, entrepreneurs, or public servants. There are thousands of podcasts competing for great guests, so there had to be an art to our ask. When my staff sent out podcast requests in the beginning of my program, they were basic, blanket emails requesting guests. That strategy has evolved over time. As we recorded more shows, and booked more high-profile guests, in the process we built our confidence about who else we could ask. When we send an email request today, we make sure to give many specifics about the program, making sure to explain who we have had on the show so that future guests know they are in good company.

I originally booked Mark Cuban, whom I knew, and built on that. I had met Mark when I did a stint on *Shark Tank*, but I didn't know him personally. Still, I called him and asked for some business advice, which he graciously offered. As we talked, I mentioned my podcast, and he agreed to be a guest. It's not that I'm telling you to call Mark Cuban. There is more than one way to reach people. Most of us have social media accounts, and most well-known business people have them and read them—especially, in my experience, Instagram messages. You can message just about anyone on Instagram. Or find the person who works with or for the person you want to reach, and see if you can talk to them. The point is, organize yourself, prepare, and get yourself noticed. Find a way in. There is always a way.

After Mark Cuban, I booked Paris Hilton, whom I also knew— I was a nanny for her and her sister Nicky when they were just schoolgirls! Those two guests, Mark and Paris, helped get my podcast off the ground. After I had an exchange on Twitter with Hillary Clinton, she agreed to be on the show! My team and I kept chipping away at booking interesting guests, and we continue to do so today. We reached out to Facebook's Sheryl Sandberg and asked her to be on my podcast, and she said yes. The more people who said yes, the more willing other people were to come on. Eventually we made it into the top five podcasts, and we built on that achievement to book more high-quality guests. If you don't ask, you don't get.

Set yourself up for success by having your pitch ready, and know what questions you want to ask. Lay the groundwork. Do your homework. Then when you call whoever it is that you need to call, you will sound like someone worth listening to. Show you know what you're talking about. Make it personal. We make sure to tell prospective guests that we are not political, we are not Republican or Democrat. Our only goal is to have interesting conversations with fascinating guests from across all social and political spectrums and share those discussions with our listeners. We also want to make sure our guests feel that they're walking into a room with good people.

Setting myself up for success was crucial to eventually getting cast on *The Apprentice: Martha Stewart* in 2005. This was preceded by an earlier attempt to get cast on the original *Apprentice* with Donald Trump. At the time, I didn't know how to use a video camera, let alone appear coherent on film. I didn't even understand what the show was about. Plus, I thought there would be hundreds of thousands of people vying for the same opportunity and that my chances would be slim to none. I did it anyway. I got hold of a simple video camera, taught myself how to use it, did my own hair and makeup, practiced what I was going to say and how I would say it, and recorded myself. I sent in the video, and the process started. I could have just sat around and talked about doing it, but instead, I got up off the couch, taught myself what I needed to know about putting together an entry package, did it, and sent in the application. I did the work required to the best of my ability. If I hadn't, as I'll explain later, my stint on Martha's version would never have happened.

If I am going to get into a new business or a new marketing space and I want to be successful, especially if I am going to be the face of the product, I want it to be the best it can be. Due diligence is crucial.

Not that long ago, I worked up the nerve to call film producer and media mogul Jeffrey Katzenberg to talk to him about a business in which he was an investor and I also had an interest, the travel points business. The Jeffrey Katzenberg call started with my obsession with travel miles and points you earn various ways, through credit cards usually, and the fear of dying with unused points. It's a forgotten currency that few understand. Points might be seen as the ultimate in stacking, earning credits for more travel each time you get on a plane, buy something with your credit card, or stay at a hotel. At any rate, there are many people who have so many points from credit cards and other rewards programs who don't exploit them when you should be in it to win it with your points. I asked smart people about how they used their travel points, and it turns out that many of them don't know how to use them well either.

In general, many people find points too much trouble to figure out, or they forget they have them, or they don't know how to use them to maximize their value. For instance, if you book with one card or through a certain website you might earn $1.80 from your points, and if you book in another way, you'll get only a dollar for your points. Does your head hurt yet? Points *can* be complicated to figure out. There are so many different deals and bonuses you can get from so many different points. Yet there is no one place that aggregates information about what points are worth and the best ways to use them. As a consequence, there are probably billions of unused points out there, just languishing. That is a problem I could solve. Somehow, without knowing anything about it, I wanted to be in the points business.

The first thing I did was to look up points online, just to see if there was a travel agent or anyone who specialized in point accumulation and strategic use. There are people in the travel space who are famous for points, but they don't make the information about it that digestible.

I did some digging and found somebody who was written up in *Condé Nast Traveler* who seemed to be an expert on the points business. I was interested in talking to this man about booking a European trip, but I also wanted to understand his business. I reached out to him on Instagram, where he had few followers, and we talked. He explained how he runs his points business. At a certain point during our conversation, I brought in my fiancé, Paul, and a friend of mine who is a good business person and something of a point savant. After the conversation ended, my friend told me she was not impressed with the point expert. She didn't come from a place of yes. I don't think it's a good idea to be too quick to judge, especially when all the information necessary to make a fair judgment is not available. I wanted to give him the benefit of the doubt and kept pushing through. I wanted to be in the points business.

If you don't ask, you don't get.

The points person had a company that needed investors in order to complete seed funding, or the first official funding stage of a business. While Paul, my friend, and I were on the call with the points person, he mentioned Jeffrey Katzenberg and said that Katzenberg had been one of his initial investors. That was interesting, because I'm always thinking about marketing. If I was to be the face of a company, and also invest money in it, adding Jeffrey Katzenberg to the mix would give the project a little more sizzle. We could also use my existing Bethenny marketplace to build out the business, in addition to whatever site had already been built by the founder.

I actually didn't feel that I needed to call Jeffrey Katzenberg to do a deal for this points business. I did see it as a great reason to call a powerful and fairly inaccessible person and see where he stood in the business. In fact, I was teed up. First I wrote Jeffrey an introductory email. It was friendly and casual but still professional, and it had a hook. I told him I was interested in investing in a business that I had heard he was involved in. I introduced myself and told him what I was thinking about the points business and established that I had spoken to the same person he had been in touch with. I introduced the idea that we might be partners in the venture, and if he had a few minutes I'd like to chat about it. I wanted to vet the idea with him. I didn't go into too much detail in the email, because if I did, he might have felt no need to respond. I wanted to write enough to indicate I was serious but not so much that he didn't need to talk to me about it. I wanted to pique his interest. He replied instantly.

Later I told this story to Sheryl Sandberg, COO of the social media platform Facebook. I told her I couldn't believe that I had cold-called Jeffrey and that he had called me back. "Of course he would," she replied. "Why wouldn't he call you back? If you were a man, you would not be surprised or impressed that he called you back, you'd just expect it, being as successful as you are," she said. Sheryl felt that the fact that I'm a woman accounted for my surprise that a powerful man gave me the time of day. But I don't think that's it. I still think it's pretty amazing he called me back. I still think of myself as the girl living in a studio apartment. I didn't think Jeffrey would think I was important enough to reply to. So you see, I have my moments of insecurity even today. But that does not stop me from trying. I'm relentless. I want to get the ball into the end zone.

Jeffrey and I set a call for the same day. He confirmed that he was indeed interested in the business. "Of course, it's a startup and who knows what's going to happen," he told me, but he had indeed also invested in it. He closed by saying welcome aboard and that I could call him anytime for anything. Wow! I don't know where that phone call and connection will lead me in the future, but the possibilities might be endless.

B SMART

Stack It to Win It

When I talked to Jeffrey Katzenberg about a potential business partnership, in the back of my mind I was thinking, *I have to book him as a podcast guest.* What a fantastic conversation that would make! When you've had people like Sheryl Sandberg and Hillary Clinton on a podcast, booking Jeffrey Katzenberg doesn't seem like such a long shot. There I was on the phone with one of the most iconic, powerful people in media, entertainment, and moviemaking. I didn't know when I would talk to him again, but I had him on the phone. Why waste an opportunity? There is always time for one more question. In it to win it means never letting an opportunity staring you in the face get away. It's exactly how I feel about being on reality television; it's something I intrinsically understand. What is the point of being on television if you're not marketing something or monetizing it in some way beyond what you're getting paid to appear on the show? Being in it to win it means stacking. You always have to think about the potential extensions of the opportunities you come across. Every idea can hold ten more ideas on top of it—what are they? Successful people are efficient people and squeeze every drop out of the sponge.

Maintain Your Enthusiasm

TV producer, host, journalist, and friend Andy Cohen embod-ies enthusiasm. I think it's one of his secret ingredients of success. He still wants to do the work, make the call, stack the decks, and have fun while working a million miles a minute. His dream was to be in television news, perhaps as a host. When he finished college he moved to New York with that dream and had an opportunity to be an intern at CBS. "You know what," he told me, "I'm going to wait tables until I can get a job at CBS. Something has to open up." He worked his tail off as an intern and something did open up. "Weirdly, a nighttime desk assistant left the CBS morning show shortly after I moved to New York, and I got that job." He loved it. "I was working seventy hours a week but I didn't care. I worked so hard and I felt so successful because I was getting [pay]checks that said CBS on them. I just thought I was the shit. I thought I was amazing."

Andy still feels lucky, and he brings that same attitude and enthu-siasm to his work today. He is in it to win it. "I've had so many jobs. I worked at a pushcart in Faneuil Hall in Boston selling Mexican blankets. I was a waiter. I worked at a radio station. And I always worked it. I showed up." He also invested the time in his interests. "It's such simple advice, but I always say to people, if you are pas-sionate about something you should be able to succeed because the passion will drive you." That's great advice—to be in it to win it, you have to be motivated by a passion for what you want to do.

As you continue on this journey with me, remember that I started in the same place everyone else does: at the beginning. Every time I begin a new venture, I start at the beginning, with a phone call, an email, a proactive approach. This message under-pins all the other lessons in the book. Doing what it takes to make things happen is the most important tool in your box.

2

Success Is the Intersection of Intention and Luck

I'M INTENTIONAL ABOUT MY LIFE, FROM WHAT I PUT INTO MY BODY (mostly good stuff with room for aware indulgence) to prioritizing quality sleep (nonnegotiable, but I could still be better at getting enough), vacation planning (I want to relax and reignite when I'm away), spending quality time with my daughter (can't get enough!), renovating a house (organization is everything), and working on a new business. My definition of intention is made up of four parts: deliberate attention to the matter at hand; clarity about what needs to be accomplished in each area of life; conscious planning of steps needed to get there; and ruthlessness about the use of time needed. When I am rushing or feeling under pressure to perform, I'm frustrated, and that's when mistakes are made. When I stop, or give myself space, in this case to be intentional about my work, when I can truly think about it, be deliberate about it, I feel better about myself, and the work itself is of a higher quality. Intentionality holds the same power whether it's applied to parenting, running a business, cooking, throwing a party, or learning something new.

On my podcast, *Just B with Bethenny*, I often talk with my guests about the misconception that successful people are just lucky people. By the time you hear about someone's success, it can often seem as if it just happened out of the blue, and it didn't. Absolutely, luck or happenstance does have something to do with success. In fact, most of the people I talk to agree that they've been extremely lucky in business and life. Steven Madden, who revolutionized the shoe business with his eponymous company, told me that a lot of success involves recognizing a lucky break and capitalizing on it. Intention meets attention. He told me, "I believe that I had the knowledge to know when I was lucky. I always said when the window is open, jump through it. Some people get those lucky breaks and they don't take advantage of them."

For Steve, noticing opportunities came early. When he was just sixteen, he worked at a Cedarhurst, New York, shoe store called Toulouse. It opened his eyes to opportunities the fashion industry offered because he noticed that his boss was only ten years older than he was. At twenty-six, this young man owned a business and drove an expensive car! After Steve dropped out of college in Florida for poor grades (and at his father's insistence), he moved to Greenwich Village, still thinking about the fashion business. He took a job as a sales representative for L. J. Simone, a women's boot wholesaler, and realized this was a lucky break for a kid with no college degree. He worked there for nearly a decade, accepting new roles and positions along the way, and learning the shoe business—groundwork for what would eventually become his successful attempt at creating his own line of shoes. Opportunities and luck don't always come in a glamorous package. Sometimes they come in the form of a sales job. Steve knew it was an opportunity to learn about a business he was interested in.

When you are intentional, you align how you spend your time with your values and goals in your life. Intention attunes you to opportunities that will benefit your goals.

Steve makes an important point, because we all know smart people who push papers around a desk. They're like the people who "work out" every day but they actually end up screwing around by socializing or taking selfies in front of the weight machine, and their abs stay the same no matter how many trips to the gym they make. They have no intentionality about their workout. The same is true of life. If you don't seize the opportunity when it's in front of you, and focus on the task at hand, you don't get anything out of it. I've been doing yoga for probably thirty years. I see it as a metaphor for having good form and discipline no matter what you are doing. I know I can do a pose, but to get the benefit of it, I have to think about it and be fully conscious and intentional about it; otherwise, it's not doing anything for me but wasting my time. It is the same in life.

John Paul Jones DeJoria, billionaire entrepreneur and philanthropist who cofounded Paul Mitchell hair products and the Patrón Spirits Company, talked to me about luck and intention, and his spin was fascinating. "A lot of luck has to do with what you believe in. Wherever you put your energy, the more energy you put forth, along with enthusiasm for what you're doing and what you believe in, the more energy comes from the universe to you. It gives you that extra little bump and maybe that creates something that we call luck." In this case, the energy John talks about is interchangeable with intention, because intention *is* a form of energy. "And luck isn't just a roll of the dice. It has a lot to do with how you live your life, how you use your energy, what you do for others, and what you pull in," he says.

B SMART

The Power of Four

I think of intention as having four distinct and important parts:

1. **Deliberate** attention to the matter at hand. Focus on the work you are doing without distraction, and it will be done better and more efficiently.

2. **Clarity** about what needs to be accomplished in each area of life. Know and understand all the tasks necessary to get to the finish line.

3. **Conscious** planning of steps needed to get there. How will you accomplish your goals? Gather your thoughts before you begin on working toward a goal. Yes, you may need to revise as you go, but you can only know corrections and modifications if you have thought the journey through.

4. **Ruthlessness** about the use of time needed to accomplish goals. Use your time wisely! It's precious.

Get on the Right Road

During the fever pitch of the 2020 pandemic, I was staying at home just like everyone else. During that time, I made the somewhat obvious observation that no one was making as many trips to the store as they had been pre-pandemic. Many didn't want to go into public spaces for any length of time. Others had left urban areas and moved to more rural or suburban places

Go where the fish are.

where stores were farther away than a walk down a city block. These two factors meant ecommerce had morphed into something quite different in 2020 than it had been previously for many people.

Both Walmart and Amazon were bringing in additional billions of dollars in profits during the pandemic. I don't pretend to compete with those behemoths on any level, but seeing the exponential growth in online shopping made me understand that it would continue to expand in scope. While shopping online for clothing or shoes or even furniture had already become commonplace, now people were starting to buy their eggs and chicken and soap online too, or at least ordering them digitally, and then driving to a grocery store parking lot to have their orders placed in the trunk of their car before they sped away, back to the safety of their homes.

Clearly, everyday shopping was never going to be the same.

Building up my ecommerce presence would be more important than ever, and it was crucial we do it sooner rather than later, because online is where the fish were swimming and would be for the foreseeable future. I had realized two months before the serious shutdown, in January 2020, that we needed a robust online marketplace, but the effort had been stalled. I had been asking my team to help me build this online hub for a long time before that. Everyone seemed to be pushing the papers around on the desk; no one was dealing with it. That changed in early 2020: we had to become intentional about the website to capitalize on the luck of timing. I had to stop everything and put my energy toward the project. There was no doubt in my mind that if I built an ecommerce website, people would come to it. If I didn't get involved and focus on it at a granular level, it would not happen. Only with my focus on it would it get it done.

I talked to my business managers about building the site, and they told me that because of the complexity of what I was asking to be done within a short time frame, the project would cost millions of dollars *and* it wouldn't make a profit. My main intention for the site was not about making money directly from sales. The site would be my flagship store, a virtual showcase for my brand. It would tell everybody that we were serious, that we had a real business with a substantial range of products. It would be a place to find and learn about my products under one virtual roof. The website would also provide a space for me to communicate ideas and expertise with visitors, and share hacks and tips with them in a friendly, conversational format. It needed to happen; not doing it wasn't an option.

Once I—and therefore my team—became intentional about the work, even obsessed with it, the energy around the project changed. Now we had a goal, to build the site in a period of weeks. I took the steps necessary to make it happen. First, I connected with and had virtual meetings with several web designers. I must have talked to at least five developers, but I wasn't getting anywhere with them. None of them seemed to understand what I wanted to do. I felt stuck. I took a step back and talked to Paul, my fiancé, about the trouble I was having finding the right person to help. Through him, I met Jill Kravetz, a dynamic problem-solver who had built other successful ecommerce websites.

Jill told me that the site could be created with all the functionality that we wanted and needed if the links to our products directed buyers to outside websites where they could make the purchase, including the Home Shopping Network, Amazon, and others. This was not an ideal solution, because we'd be driving business away from our pages and to other sites. Yet it would allow us to collect data about who was visiting and what they were clicking on and ultimately buying, even if the purchase was not made directly from our site. The price to create the site in this fashion was also significantly less than to create a site where purchases were made directly through us: $75,000 versus $2 million. The idea wasn't what I had initially thought about in terms of my website, but it was worth considering because it would still accomplish what I wanted.

The build-out was completed in a matter of weeks, and the site was and is a success, evidenced by the continual growth in traffic, and the engagement of the hundreds of thousands of visitors we capture each day, who tend to spend more time exploring the information and products we share each time they come to the site.

I believe that when you are intentional about an idea, you become more open to creative and unconventional ways of bringing it to life. Had I not followed where the fish were swimming, and become fully focused and deliberate about getting the web project done, I might have never met Jill, and I might have been less inclined to listen to her.

Stop. Take a step back.

Get Clear on Your Purpose

While intention is deliberate attention on making something happen, purpose is the "why" that underpins our goals. We can have the best intentions in the world, but if we don't know *why* we want to make the effort to do something, the results can fall short. The connection between intention and purpose was a challenge when my team and I were getting a handle on our social media marketing. Social media is necessary for brands today, but it is often a challenge for business people to do it well, because it's constant and ever-evolving. If you are running a business posting multiple times a day to Instagram, TikTok, Twitter, and Facebook (to name a few), it doesn't make a lot of practical sense. It's a game for young people who are not running businesses, and who approach social media much more intuitively than older people. For us, it presents a learning curve fraught with the possibility for error and embarrassment. I wanted to avoid mistakes, so I had to clarify the purpose of my use of various social media platforms in order to use each one effectively.

The people who excel at social media seem to be the most obsessed with it. It's impressive to see how Instagram influencers, YouTubers, and TikTok performers take such care to ensure their pictures look great and their videos professional, even though a great deal of quality social media is done with basic equipment and without a huge financial investment. Some of the most successful social media personalities are young, some in their teens and early twenties. Remarkable. They produce high-quality material because they understand the platforms and their audiences, and they are clear on what they want to accomplish with the technology. Many young people derive a great deal of personal satisfaction from creating social media content, and if they can generate an audience and turn their efforts into something bigger, like a sustainable business or brand, bravo! But I have an existing business to run, a philanthropic organization to shepherd, and a child to raise. I don't have time to obsess over social media posts. For me, it seemed like a time suck.

I had to change my thinking, because in today's world social media engagement is an absolute necessity for businesses—it's where the fish are. They aren't reading magazines or newspapers and they aren't watching television. If I was going to invest time and resources into social media, I had to be clear on the purpose of my content: to generate involvement with my brand and products through fun and engaging posts that also offer useful information and ideas.

My frustration was in pulling together the right team of people who could help me create content that was authentic to me, and not copycatting anyone else. Yes, social media has to be entertaining to be engaging, but I also want to be taken seriously as a businesswoman. This is where social media for business people becomes layered, and therefore somewhat challenging. I don't want to do social media to show off my personal life unless it is relevant to a product I want to share with followers, or if it's humorous and engaging but relevant to who I am. I am most interested in creating posts around business, entrepreneurship, food, and other topics that are of interest to me. And rarely if ever do I filter myself.

I remember one person on my team telling me, "If you want to do well on social media, post more of those funny videos you did with vodka and music." My frustration with that concept is that those types of posts seem gimmicky to me, and that's not who I am. I felt that my posts had to be compelling and tell stories that are authentic to me. Other people can be totally inauthentic on Instagram or TikTok and it works for them, but it would not work for me. There is a tendency among marketers and others who do social media professionally to advise their clients to rely on current trends and what everybody else is doing, and that's fundamentally not who I am. I don't want to do things that make me feel inauthentic or are riding someone else's wave.

One factor that helped me focus on purpose was the understanding that social media doesn't have to look perfect. Although the photography should look good, especially of food, since I'm a chef, and any information and instructions must be accurate and useful, the actual execution of the content can be informal. That's true to me, so I could use that aspect of TikTok to my advantage because informality allows for humor. I can be silly in my pajamas because that's who I am. I'm not doing fashion. I'm not interested in showing myself made up and coiffed to within an inch of my life, which to me feels like low-hanging fruit. That's not on brand for me. I want to show what I do, how I look, within the environment of my brand and business.

If I don't have the time for it to come from my own voice, how am I supposed to accomplish it? Sometimes you have to take a step back and tackle the message you want to convey from another angle, or with another tactic. I talked to Jill, who built my marketplace, about the problem. She suggested I hire a young person who was experienced with TikTok to help with the posts for that platform. I understood where she was coming from, but TikTok is just one of many social media outlets I use. My feeling was that we should be posting business information on that and all my social media platforms, in a cohesive, holistic way. I didn't think I needed a young person to tell me how to dance to music. I felt working with someone who was focused on making silly dances was going to put me in a position of chasing relevancy. That wasn't going to help me with what I was trying to accomplish. Focusing on frivolous activities seemed lacking in dignity and integrity for me and had nothing to do with running a multi-million-dollar business.

It was a real dilemma, because using TikTok the way I wanted to use it, to share business information, was a fairly new concept. TikTok was originally geared toward young kids, ages nine to thirteen. When the platform first came on the scene, many people told me that it wasn't going to move from that space and demographic, but I thought differently. I could see that the format had potential applications for business, so the advice to stay away from it was bad. Just as Facebook morphed from a way for college kids to keep tabs on one another into a vehicle for baby boomers and businesses to connect, TikTok was poised to become useful for sharing information that went beyond silly dances.

I looked at how other people I admired were using the platform, which helped me understand its potential. Different people approach social media in ways that work for them—and that way may not work for me. I watched Mark Cuban sitting down in a simple video, just saying hey, here are the three ways I learned about business. The video may not have been slick, but the content was compelling and useful. He wasn't doing a schtick. I watched another fantastic business coach use the medium to talk about the way he helps teams win—practical, engaging information. Most of the successful business people on the platform weren't allowing themselves to get stuck in a false idea of what TikTok was: they were making TikTok into what *they* wanted and needed it to be. You have to use social media in the ways that work for you. Don't allow what has already been done on social media to dictate what you do with it. Figure out what works for you.

Brooke Shields and I talked about social media and TikTok in particular, and she said something that confirmed how I look at it. "It's how you approach it," she said. "At first I refused to do it. I didn't want to take a picture of my food; I didn't think people needed to know what I was eating. I also didn't want to go down the rabbit hole of time it takes." Exactly my feeling. Then Brooke realized she was actually losing jobs to social media influencers and understood it was a necessary part of her business as an entrepreneur and an actress with new projects on the horizon.

She said her thoughts about it evolved as she started to use it more regularly. "I am in a different mindset about it now. I found the career purpose for TikTok. I could show a behind-the-scenes look at the film I was shooting in Scotland, for example. I could

31

let people in on the fantasy of riding a horse through the Scottish countryside. My social media became so much more purposeful." Brooke and I are both using TikTok for what it can do for our brands and businesses—we're molding the technology to serve us, not the other way around. "It's another outlet to me," she says. It's another way to be creative, to be herself. "I may edit out an unflattering photo, and I do want to get a good angle, but I never use a heavy hand to erase every last laugh line." She is focused on portraying what she is doing realistically. Smart.

The kind of content we needed to post—great tips, and I have plenty of them—felt right. Under that umbrella, TikTok made sense. It just felt so wrong to be told that I should be paying attention to what's on trend and what's cool—because that can change on a dime tomorrow.

I didn't need a social media person who would tell me the best times to post a picture of myself in a bathing suit with a cute, kitschy caption. What I needed was someone who understood the idea of sharing useful business content in a catchy, engaging way, and who could own the process. Someone who can say, let's post a business video on Monday, and a food video on Tuesday, and on Thursday or Friday let's do financial tips because those days are paydays for a lot of people. Let's think about the timing of information and give people the right tips when they need them.

We had been tackling social media from the top down, instead of from the bottom up. Jill asked whether I needed a social media producer. All of a sudden, the light bulb went on over both our heads. We looked at each other, and said no, we actually don't. Going forward, I told my assistant exactly what I wanted, which can be overwhelming because I have several accounts. So I said to her that it's not an emergency, it's social media. When we decide to post something, we'll make sure it's good. If we don't have a good post, we won't do it. That helped put social media in perspective, and allowed us some freedom to focus on quality over quantity.

Sometimes you have to get some perspective, look at something one way and then go upside down and figure out how to match your purpose with the materials you have to work with. You can be swimming your hardest, but if you go in the wrong direction, it doesn't make a difference. The finish line is behind you.

B SMART

Go In, Go Deep to Find Your Intention

I've been practicing yoga on and off for more than thirty years. I don't do it all the time, but I make my best effort to have some consistency. For me, it's a place where fitness, relaxation, and spirituality meet. It is therapeutic, centering, and emotionally and physically strengthening. Yoga also helps me focus on my intention. Recently I made it a priority to practice my yoga routine in the morning, for forty-five minutes, right out of bed, in my pajamas. Since I do it at home, there's no need to put on a fancy yoga outfit (which I wouldn't do anyway, even if I was going to a high-end yoga studio in Manhattan). I roll out my yoga mat and start my routine with a simple meditation that includes focused breathing while listening to a meditation app. Then I ease into my yoga moves, paying close attention to my form, working through each pose consciously.

It sounds like I'm peaceful, but many times the thoughts are still rolling! My mornings are always different. I'm not perfect. I don't eat the same thing every day, but if I feel I have been toxic in the way I have been eating I do make an effort to start the next day cleaner. I let my dogs out, take some vitamins, and perhaps make an iced coffee or drink a matcha latte. I sometimes eat breakfast

33

late, usually after eleven a.m., which can include a protein like an omelet. My schedule, which is different every day, dictates where I am and what I do, but easing into the morning with yoga helps set me up for success during the day, and it helps me set my own intentions for the day and remain intentional until I tuck into bed at night.

There is a great deal of research that shows that even twenty-five minutes a day of yoga or mindfulness meditation increases brain function, improves focus, and leads to less tendency to have knee-jerk reactions to the minor and major annoyances and challenges of your day. Try it, and see what happens. You may not have a spiritual awakening, but you could well feel more prepared to take on projects with a renewed vigor. You may notice that you are more fully in the moment and effective as you work on projects, take care of the kids, shop, cook, clean, or whatever.

Get to the Root of the Issue

If you keep moving forward but without the proper intention, you could end up damaging your business, brand, or personal life. Once you are intentional and know your purpose, it's much easier to identify what is holding you back. That way, when something doesn't seem as if it's working, you're not putting a Band-Aid on it and hoping for the best. Instead, you can get to the root of the problem and pull it out just as you would in any area of your life. If you find a small leak in a wall, you don't just plug it up. You find the source of the leak and fix it. If your skin is chronically breaking out, you can't just put ointment on

> You have to get to the root of the problem, and pull it out.

it, forget about it, and go back to business as usual. It's likely a sign that something is amiss with your health, your diet, or your sleep or stress levels, and you can make changes in those areas. If your child is misbehaving, you can't simply issue a punishment and expect that to fix the problem. My daughter knows when I punish her it's for real; I don't bluff. A slap on the hand is not a replacement for the hard work and intentionality of conscious parenting, which includes digging deeply to find the cause of your child's behavior. It is the same when building a business, marketplace, or social media presence: you have to take a step back, focus your intention and purpose, get to the core of what is going wrong, and solve the problem from the base. Intention and purpose is all bottom up, not top down.

Make sure to check back in with yourself. Ask yourself, is this (job, pursuit, etc.) working? Is it happening in the way I want it to happen? If I'm working out at the gym every day, am I seeing results? If I'm parenting, am I seeing my child thriving, are they happy at school, engaged socially, feeling good? If I'm working in business, am I seeing results in terms of sales or customers?

Look around. If you see a school of fish, go toward those fish. If you see something that seems to be headed in the same direction you want to go in, get in the current and go with the flow.

3

Trust the Process

PEOPLE—JOURNALISTS, FANS, EVEN FRIENDS—OFTEN ASK ME,
what's next? Do you feel that you've made it now and you can
relax? Honestly, I am not a person who makes big, grand plans
because, well, plans have a way of falling through or changing.
When you act in a way that is intentional and purposeful, you
then have to trust the process without being wedded to a specific
outcome. Comedian Howie Mandel told me a few years ago that
in 2003 he was thinking of leaving the entertainment business. He
had been asked to host the game show *Deal or No Deal*, but had
declined the offer more than once. He ultimately decided to try
it—including after some persuasion from his wife—and it changed
his life and career forever, in a positive way. He now has a major
career. The point is, when you are on the path, keep going and see
where it takes you. You *can* change course if necessary, but only if
you are actually on the road!

Instead of planning a future that hinges on a single desired result, I trust the process. No one is bigger than the game—you have to let life play out and trust that if you're doing the right things, you will get where you want to go. By that I mean that I keep doing what is necessary to run my businesses, enjoy life, and raise my daughter. I am aware of what's going on in front of me. I look at all the signs, and that involves thinking and analysis. It's not that I think everything is going to work out without any effort on my part—there's always work involved. What I *don't* do is get caught up in worrying about the future. If I do the work and put one foot in front of the other, the process is going to work. What is supposed to happen will happen.

When I sold the cocktail portion of my business to Beam in 2011, I could have stopped working and relaxed. Before that happened, despite being on a couple of television shows, I was still broke. The Beam deal was the biggest thing that had ever happened to me to that point. I created the Skinnygirl margarita, a low-calorie ready-to-drink cocktail, in my kitchen because I enjoyed having a cocktail but I didn't want to consume all the sugar and calories that are associated with the cocktails I liked best, like a classic margarita. The best ideas are often the simplest ones that other people tend to overlook because they just seem too obvious.

The margarita became a huge hit not long after we brought it to market in 2009. I wasn't surprised by the interest in the cocktail because I knew that I had tapped into a need in the market that wasn't being served. I had solved a problem primarily for women, who to this point went largely underserved (no pun intended) in the spirits industry. The liquor business is primarily run by and marketed to men. Women are often an afterthought. My margarita drink was targeted to women; it gave them something they could feel good about enjoying. The deal I made with Beam a few years after the cocktail hit the market was so unusual it made the cover of *Forbes*. It was *that* extraordinary. A lot of money was involved. I could have bought a small island and stayed there. But I didn't.

I don't make decisions because of money, or only based on money. I make decisions around ideas. I'm addicted to them—I'm an idea hamster! Not only do I constantly come up with new things, I am compelled to execute them. An idea is nothing if it just sits there. Execution is everything. In chapter one, I talked about doing the work, being in the game in a proactive way, but once you're in the game you have to trust the process, wherever it may take you.

There have been many other times in my life when I've had to do this. I wrote my first book, *Naturally Thin*, in 2009, and it was on the *New York Times* bestseller list for five months. When I first had the idea, my representatives who were helping me sell the book mentioned one major publisher of diet books. They were skeptical this publisher would buy it because my book didn't promise a quick fix. Other publishers felt the same. At the time, diet books were focused on time frames and eating plans, as in lose ten pounds in ten days, or twenty-one-day food fixes, and so on. I was ahead of the curve in terms of talking about creating a healthy relationship with food versus a specific eating plan. My book was about the emotionality of food and how you live with food in a healthy way. This is now a common and accepted idea, but at the time, talking about balance and emotion in a diet book was too new.

Naturally Thin came from an emotional place in me. It dealt with the feelings I have about food, what I call food noise, and that I know other people have too. It was a holistic approach that no diet books at the time were taking. That is different today, but back in 2009 it seemed like a risk to publishers because it broke the mold. I wrote the book and eventually found a publisher. I trusted that the book would reach its audience once it was published, and it did, as I knew it would because it tapped into the emotional aspect of eating, which women in particular recognize, experience, and struggle with. I knew that following through with the idea for the book, sitting down and writing it, finding a publisher, talking about it and promoting it—all that was going to create the right kind of progress, even if there were times when it didn't always look as if progress was being made.

B SMART

Enjoy the Journey

Business and life are about the journey. That is an important idea and a big part of the mental effort it takes to be successful. Trusting the process lets you enjoy that journey and learn from it. See it as an exciting trip, because it is. The journey is never going to be what you thought it was going to be—it's actually more interesting. As you lay the groundwork for whatever you're doing, one brick at a time, remember you're not eating the meal in one mouthful. Take one bite at a time, put one foot in front of the other, and you will get there. Some of the steps you're taking can feel as if they have nothing to do with what you want to do or where you want to go.

For instance, early in my career when I produced large events, all the details such as lighting, budget, music, sound, and so on didn't seem relevant to what I do today, when in fact, they have everything to do with where I am now: caring about the details, understanding all the facets that create a successful event, has also helped me create a successful business. When I had to hustle in my baked goods business, I did everything I needed to do to get my baking business off the ground: I developed the recipes; tested and perfected them; identified the market; baked and packaged the goods; distributed them to stores or private clients; and applied for and was cast on a reality show that I felt would help promote the brand. None of this resulted in the kind of national boutique healthy baking business I had envisioned. But I never stopped moving forward, meeting or calling the next person, creating a new idea, and telling people about it. The problem-solving skills I learned from that experience and so many others still help me today.

Relax into the steps you are taking to reach a goal, because everything will teach you something. If you remain completely open about what is happening in the process, you will see new opportunities.

That doesn't mean that when something hasn't worked out, I wasn't upset. Yes, I've often felt disappointment, but it's never deterred me or made me think for a second that the process wasn't playing out and I should not keep going with the work and my intention. This is true for work as much as it is for relationships, and any passions or interests you have. I've been disappointed, but I also always have a gut instinct that whatever is happening has a reason behind it and something to teach me. This has included the worst moments in my life, such as being broke in Manhattan while trying to get a baking business off the ground, and my nightmare divorce.

I also know that something else great will come along: a new idea forms, a new opportunity comes my way, or I see something in a new way—if I do the work and trust the process. I don't deny any of my feelings, good or bad, because I know that I will come out on the other side of them. Tomorrow is another day.

I tested this idea after I missed being cast on the second season of the original *Apprentice*. I was living in a tiny apartment on the

Upper East Side of Manhattan, with no safety net, no money, and a wheat- and dairy-free baked goods business that was in free fall. I'd bake cookies all night in borrowed spaces because I could not afford to rent an automated commercial bakery. I'd package up the cookies when they were done baking and get them ready for delivery the next day. In the morning I'd deliver the treats all over the city in my awful car with a cracked windshield. I was always working. An acquaintance told me about *The Apprentice* with Donald Trump. It had already aired for one season, and it was casting season two. This person said I would never get on the show, which seemed like a dare, so I applied. I imagined that *The Apprentice* would be my ticket out.

There are many hoops you have to jump through to get on a reality show like *The Apprentice*: psychological testing, sequestering, lots of questions, repeated auditions. It's emotionally and physically demanding, but I wanted to be on the show so badly, I was willing to endure it. On the last day of casting for the original show—I had made it *that* far—the producers came into my hotel room at the DoubleTree in Los Angeles. I had watched as the initial group of fifty people dwindled down to about twenty. I was pretty confident the producer was coming to tell me I had made the cut. Instead, he said, "You didn't make it. You're the first alternate." Ouch.

> No one is bigger than the game.

Right after that rejection I went to the Kentucky Derby, which is a high-profile, exciting event that can be hard to get into. I was able to get in because I had grown up around racetracks and knew many people in that world. I was hoping to go there triumphant at being cast on a hit reality show. Instead, I stayed in a second-rate hotel and tried my best to enjoy myself and have fun even though I was depressed about going through all the casting trials and still

getting sent home. I also went back to
my life trying to sell cookies, *and* trying
to get on television.

> I make decisions
> around ideas.

Even though it hurt, I was not going
to miss out on any opportunities that being involved in the show
gave me. After the first time I didn't make the cut, I realized that I
now knew a few people in the television business, and more importantly, they knew me. I had developed a great rapport with many
of the people involved in the first nightmare casting exercise. I was
smart enough to maintain contact with the casting agents for the
show. I'd check in with them periodically, not in an annoying way
but in a friendly, hey-it's-Bethenny-I'm-here kind of way. I did it
often enough so they knew I was out there and interested in opportunities, but not so much that they dreaded seeing my name in
their inboxes.

A couple of years later, the casting people invited me back for
another round of the same dreadful casting experience, this time
for a new version of the show, starring Martha Stewart. The first
time I had been up for a part on the original, I was under the naïve
impression that being cast on *The Apprentice* was about demon-
strating how professional and polished you are. How good at business you are. By the time I was called for the second audition I had
come to the realization that the producers didn't necessarily care if
you're good at business. It's a television show. They want you to be
good at being on television. They wanted you to be entertaining
and fun to watch. That's quite different from being a good business
person.

We were in the initial meeting with other potential cast members, and Mark Burnett asked me why I should get a spot rather
than the woman sitting next to me. I remember remarking that she
shouldn't be cast because she had the nerve to bring a fake Marc

Jacobs bag to a job interview. I'm not even sure if this was actually true, but the bag looked cheap, and I pointed it out. I guess it was a polarizing comment. And as it turned out, that's good for TV. In 2005, I was cast on NBC's *The Apprentice: Martha Stewart*.

They were predicting that 42 million people would tune in. "It's going to be the biggest thing ever because she's getting out of prison," someone at the table said. Well...it was not a hit. Only about eleven million people watched. At the time this was considered to be a significant failure because there were not as many channels (let alone streaming) as there are today, *and* it was a network program with a large number of promotional dollars behind it, featuring a well-known and infamous host.

I finished in second place on the show. That hurt, because I truly believed that my life and business prospects were going to be changed by this experience. I thought just being on television would lead to immediate success. Winning would have been the real ticket out of the rat trap I was living in. My cookie business would finally take off. None of those boxes got checked.

No matter what anyone may tell you, first runner up is not a ticket to anywhere. No one cares who comes in second. Good things didn't just spontaneously "happen" after the show was over. Two years later I was still baking cookies and driving them around New York in the same awful green Bronco. But you know what? I trusted. I kept working and connecting. I kept *going*. The experience taught me that it's not enough to get yourself in the door. Getting in the door is great, but it's not enough. It's what you do next that matters.

The backdrop of my life stayed the same for a long time: I had no money, a crummy apartment, and I was still busting my butt. I had no choice but to be in the process, and trust it. I was doing everything I could do. I was seeing what was going on around me, and I was making decisions. I would study for hours and hours just to be booked on the *Today* show to talk about healthy baking and cooking. I just wanted to *be something*. I was also trying to pitch a cooking show, begging various TV agents to represent me. I knew somebody who knew somebody who was at the William Morris Agency (WMA), and I was able to talk to them, but they wouldn't represent me. I thought being on Martha's *Apprentice* was going be such a big deal, but nobody seemed to care or even remember. The lesson for me is that sometimes we don't understand the assignment. The real lesson of being on that show was to learn about being entertaining on television, and to establish relationships that I could build on for my next attempt at TV.

One day I was having dinner at a restaurant called Nobu in Manhattan. The person I was with pointed out that John Walsh, the host of *America's Most Wanted* at the time, was there eating with his agent, Lance Klein, who was at WMA (this was before they merged with Endeavor and became WME). I walked over to the table and introduced myself. Yes, it took a little courage, but my motivation to make a connection helped me overcome any nervousness or doubt I may have felt. I was friendly, and told Lance that I needed an agent. I guess I was convincing—or maybe he admired my bravado—because he agreed to talk to me. I sold him on myself.

I had an idea for a cooking show that I described as cooking meets *Survivor*. High stakes cooking. At the same time that I was pitching my show idea, I was still trying to get my wheat-, egg-, gluten-, and dairy-free cookie business off the ground. One time I remember going out to the Hamptons in the summer wearing my Juicy Couture terry cloth romper, and handing out my baked goodies at polo matches. I had tried to get the cookies into gift bags or swag bags that were handed out to VIP guests at the polo matches. I actually would have preferred to stay home because I'm not terribly social. Going to these parties and networking was work, and exhausting. It was not partying for me. But again—trust the process. Staying home would not get me anywhere.

At this polo match, I ran into entrepreneur and designer Jill Zarin (also a former Housewife), whom I'd met earlier at a movie premiere. She had seen me on *The Apprentice* and liked what I had done on the show. Since we had connected in a casual, friendly way, it was nice to run into her. She approached me and said, "What are you doing, you skinny bitch? How did you get a VIP bracelet?" We laughed and started talking. Then she told me about a show Bravo was casting called *Manhattan Moms*, a reality show about moms trying to get their kids into fancy private schools. I didn't understand the idea or how I would fit into it. Besides, all I wanted to do was get on the Food Network. And, at that point, I was not a mother.

At the same time, I was watching the Food Network obsessively, writing down the names of production companies as they scrolled by at the end of any given show. I'd also try to get Bob Tuschman, head of programming at the Food Network at the time, on the phone. I didn't know that you had to go through a network production company to get approval for a show from the network. You can't just do a deal with a production company. At one point I did get Tuschman on the phone, and he told me something to the effect of, "Stop having production shows pitch us. It's never going to happen, you're not getting a show on the Food Network." Okay.

I would try to go to the South Beach Food and Wine Festival in Florida each year to meet people and network. More often than not I could not afford the trip or the ticket in. I couldn't get into an event called the Food Network Burger Bash either, because the tickets cost $500. I used to call the man who ran the event to see if I could get in. I would have died to go because people like Rachael Ray and Bobby Flay would be there, cooking burgers in a food festival–like setting. It would have meant a chance to rub elbows with so many famous chefs. I just couldn't afford it.

Back to the party: Jill said she wanted me to meet the producers of this mom-based reality show, who were at the same event. The show sounded like a train wreck to me, and I had already been on *The Apprentice*. At that time, producers didn't want people who already had a preexisting TV profile, afraid that audiences wouldn't buy into someone who had already been on television. That's funny now, because everyone on a reality show today is an actor (now called "the talent").

> It's not enough to get yourself in the door. It's what you do next that matters.

Bravo had cast four women but ultimately would not do the show if there was not a fifth mom. They had met every seemingly wealthy woman willing to be on what potentially could be train wreck TV. I was skeptical. It was an unproven genre. I also had a boyfriend at the time who didn't want to be on television—and he would by necessity have to be on the show. In other words, I would have had to break up with him if I were to do the show, because if we were together I couldn't just hide him in the closet. I could not force him to do it. It seems strange to have to decide between staying with a boyfriend and doing a reality show.

The Bravo producer also talked to me about this new show at the party. I listened but I was thinking about my cookies and my cooking show. Producer and actor Lance Bass was also at the event.

I still remember how good he smelled, because he was wearing Kiehl's musk. I know that smell and love it. I wanted to get his information so I could send him cookies. *That* was what I was focused on.

For a month, I said no. I found out later that Jen O'Connell, head of the production company for the show, had seen me on *The Apprentice: Martha Stewart.* I guess there was something about me that she and her husband, who was also a TV executive, found compelling. Jen also kept after the show's producer, Andy Cohen, to cast me, but he said no, because I had already been on a reality show. As I said, at the time, being cast on more than one reality show wasn't done. All of this was happening behind the scenes, unbeknownst to me. I was still just trying to sell cookies and get a cooking show.

After a month, I thought about the fact that it wasn't easy to get on television and perhaps I should consider the show. If it failed, it wouldn't matter, because no one would see or remember my part in it—I learned that lesson from being on Martha's *Apprentice.* But if it was successful . . . that could work in my favor. I called the producers and asked them if they were still looking for another cast member. They said yes, and I shot a couple of scenes. Bravo fell in love with me.

At the same time, my new agent and I were trying to sell a cooking-meets-*Survivor* show. We went in to pitch it to Bravo, and the people at the pitch meeting stopped and said, aren't you on this other show, referring to *Manhattan Moms.* We said, sort of, because while I was filming some shows I had not yet signed a contract and had no official deal. The cooking show was my real passion. I also thought *Manhattan Moms* was going to be a big mess. One of the people at the meeting freaked out a little, because she said I was supposed to be shooting this other show for Bravo, and why had I not signed a contract for both? This was another way that I broke a barrier, because that meeting with Bravo made a light go off. After that, the network became much more intentional about making sure no one was filming a show without having signed a contract. But at the time, I *hadn't* signed a contract. As far as I was concerned, it was not a done deal and I was a free agent. She went back to Bravo executives and asked them how I did not have a contract, along with mentioning the fact that I was pitching another show.

At that point Bravo rushed the contract through for a show that was no longer about moms but had morphed into *Real Housewives*. And that's how my part in the *Housewives* happened. It wasn't what I had been planning or trying to do, but it would ultimately open new doors for me and become my launchpad.

Nothing gets done by relaxing. I never stopped. Trusting the process means you keep taking steps every day toward a goal, and believing it's going to work, it's going to happen. Things on the side of that goal may happen that are even better, so don't discount something because it doesn't fit a rigid idea of how things are supposed to turn out. I was trying to get my cookie business off the ground, and I was taking steps to make that happen, which led somewhere else—and at the time I was willing to go there, and it ended up being bigger than what I had originally imagined or thought I had wanted.

Starting a business, being an entrepreneur is not a clear path. It's not like going to law school, passing the bar, and getting a job in a law firm, where every year there are clear steps to reaching a particular point (and even then, you have to trust the process). When you're doing something on your own, flying without a net, you're closer to nothing and everything. You have no idea if you're swimming in the right direction until you arrive. You could be in your own version of *The Poseidon Adventure*, where the boat is upside down, and you're thinking it is right side up.

Keep doing all the things necessary to get where you are going and believe they will lead you in the right direction. If something is not working, try something else. As long as you are intentional and positive and pay attention to what is working and what isn't, pivoting when necessary, you will get there.

4

Say What You Mean, Mean What You Say

I HAVE SO MUCH GOING ON IN MY LIFE, BETWEEN BUILDING MY brand, philanthropy, raising my daughter, and maintaining important relationships, I don't have time to waste. I'm direct, I'm determined, and I'm a doer. If I were the mayor of New York City, believe me, the subways would run on time. I'd make an excellent grumpy general. Maybe that's an exaggeration—maybe not—but I attribute my efficiency in great part to the fact that I do my best to be direct and make myself clear. I don't waste words or time on small talk, especially when I'm focused on important business and personal matters. Not only does this strategy eliminate confusion and misunderstandings, it also catches people off guard, you get where you're going faster, and it earns you respect. I'm known for my directness and standing by my word. People know that when I say something, I am not bluffing. If I say I'm going to do something, I do it. If I don't like the job someone has done, I am honest about it. Respectful, but real.

Efficient, effective communication is a learnable skill that starts with transparency and candor. Here's an example. I have a term for people who are rigid about sticking to plans, or have anxiety about plans coming to fruition. I call them Plan Stalkers. They drive me crazy, first because I don't like to be shackled to schedules or feel that I have to show up somewhere unless it is for a work obligation. I just like to keep things loose; not in the sense that I show up late or blow people off, because I don't. I'm always on time, and I respect other people's time. What I don't want to do is feel obliged to check in with people I have plans with. If I say I'll be somewhere, I'll be there, unless something unexpected happens.

I was planning to attend a Friday night book party that Michael Gelman, the executive producer of *Live with Kelly and Ryan*, had invited me to. It was for his wife's book. I am a friend of the show, of Kelly Ripa's, and a friend of Gelman, so I wanted to be there for his wife. They have helped me, and I knew if I was at the party it would help her promote the book. Another friend asked me to do something on the same Friday night. I said I couldn't do it because I had this other plan. She said that they were not doing anything, and to let her know if the event ended early.

I said, "Okay, but I can't promise anything and I don't want to hold you up, but I will let you know." The event was a lot of fun and ended before dinnertime. Since Paul and I were dressed and feeling good, we decided to text my friend to let her know we could have dinner if she was still available. She and her husband made an eight o'clock reservation at a restaurant near the event. Paul and I agreed to meet my friend and her husband there. Plan made.

At about twenty minutes to eight, my phone started to blow up with texts from my friend. "Where are you? What are you doing? When will you be here?" The texts didn't let up—Paul was getting them too—and finally I answered the phone and said, "*WHAT?* We are five minutes away!" Later, I told her that we had to talk about the situation. My friend claimed it was her husband's doing, but I didn't accept that. "You've been doing this for decades, and you have to stop. I can't make plans with you anymore if you're going to stalk me like this." It was a Plan Stalker Intervention. I was clear, direct, firm, but friendly. After all, she's an old and dear friend. But I meant what I said. She knew it. As a result I've been able to make so many plans with her because she doesn't stalk me about them anymore. Rant over!

Ugh! I know it can be hard and scary to be direct around difficult subjects: *I might hurt their feelings! They'll be mad at me! I'll lose out!* You have to get over that kind of thinking. Take the emotion and fear out of your conversations. Yelling and screaming are not power poses. It's time to start shooting straight and being clear about what you want. Of course, you have to know what you want before you say it—before you enter talking, don't let foggy thinking hold your words hostage. If you're concerned about something that's happening at work or home, think it through, address it directly and politely, don't bluff, and do not, under any circumstances, give ultimatums. Threats are a communication strategy for losers, not winners.

A reputation for honesty and forthrightness is a power position in any kind of negotiation, whether it's for dinner with a friend, negotiating a contract, or doing a real estate deal. Let's say you are selling your house. If I say X amount is what I'm selling my house for, I am not going to agree to a price that's far below that number. Of course, I've also done my homework, and I know what the right number should be. It's not as if I'm pulling dream numbers out of the sky. If I have done the necessary research to arrive at a price, I am not going to play games.

This gives me leverage and reduces the chance that I'll waste my time with lowball offers. Likewise, when I am buying a property, I know the market and have a price that I want to pay, and not a dollar more. I do not lie about these numbers, and I do not get emotional about a negotiation if it does not work out. I know there is always another opportunity. As a result of this strategy, which is at its core honest and direct, I have made many more good real estate deals than bad ones.

Say you're in a hard place with a negotiation of any kind, and there is a chance you won't get everything you want. First, you have to decide what's important to you. Weigh the pros and cons of saying yes to something that is not 100 percent what you envisioned. Remember too that good deals are not just about money. You can find other gives in a deal, and you also hold gives that can be offered. Find all the benefits of a deal, and add them up. Sometimes it can be worth it to say yes, depending on what your long-term goals are— temporary concessions *can* lead to future long-range wins.

Let's stick with real estate here. Say you are looking for a large house to accommodate a family and a home business. Maybe space is more important in this case than an exact location. You find the right size property and land but it may not be in the exact location you want, even though it's still a good area. It may be wise to give in on location in this situation, to get the space you need.

If you are entering into a business deal or partnership, look beyond the money on the table. Maybe there is a royalty involved that will make you more in the long run. Or maybe someone offers you less for a product you have developed, but can bring it to market faster than another entity who is promising more money up front. Money is not the only important element in a real estate or any other deal. For instance, timing might be more important to you than the cash. Be creative.

Follow Through on Your Word

I can help you figure out how to express yourself once you've made up your mind. Don't pull all your cards if you're not willing to follow through. Before you say something definitive, take a good look at the big picture and consider any and all consequences of your moves. Keep your word. If there's a chance you'll regret walking, pull back and do a deep think. I've done this many times in business and personal matters. Whether it's a deal for a new product or deciding to make a large personal purchase, there have been times when I have had to step back and give myself some time to weigh the pros and cons, do a listening tour, asking trusted advisors and experts for their opinions, experiences, and insights, and then I feel clearer about making a decision.

For example, in 2019 I started to do a deep think about walking away from the *Housewives* for the second and final time. I had left the show once before, in 2010, because I didn't feel good about taking part in the show, which I thought had become exploitative and, honestly, somewhat embarrassing. I went back to the show in 2015 because I felt it was a different show, and it was an opportunity for me to talk about what I was doing with my businesses. By 2019, a question kept popping up in my mind: Was I going to return to the *Housewives*? I didn't want to, but I was also weighing the money, the brand, and the platform, and what it offered me. This made me ask myself *why* I was still doing the *Housewives*. I had to give myself a straight answer. The last person you want to bullshit is yourself.

I had to be clear about the reason I wanted to leave. First, there were other things I wanted to do, including more philanthropic and relief work, new business ventures, and personal, family-based things. As the legendary creator of *Saturday Night Live* Lorne Michaels said to me once, you have to make an exit to make an entrance. I wanted to make a new entrance because the *Housewives* was not necessarily moving my brand forward any longer.

After I left in 2020, there was *so* much gossip about why I had walked away, most of it centering around the idea that Bravo wasn't meeting my compensation demands. That makes me laugh because the opposite was true. The *only* reason I had stayed past my personal *Housewives* expiration date was because the money was so good. I had to own up to the fact that a paycheck, no matter how fat, is ultimately not the best reason to do something you don't enjoy. You have to look at the big picture. The *Housewives* didn't feel like me anymore.

The show wasn't serving my business plans, it was not benefiting my family life, and it was not helping my brand. The only thing it was helping was my bank account. But you can't pick up every quarter on the floor—meaning sometimes it's foolish to go for the money above all else. After I came to this realization, leaving wasn't going to be easy, but it *was* a clear decision. I could breathe.

I wasn't telling them I wasn't coming back as a ploy to get more money. They had offered me great money. However, I had asked my lawyers to confirm that the offer they had made was "best and final" because it included a clause that said that they would not pay for episodes I did not appear in—Bravo had learned a lesson when two *Housewives* cast members, Lisa Vanderpump (Beverly Hills) and NeNe Leakes (Atlanta), missed several episodes but were still paid for them. The contract stipulated that I would not be paid for episodes I was not in. I didn't want to agree to that, and the producers knew that I was a hard worker. Even when my boyfriend, Dennis Shields, passed away, I was on the show three weeks later. They knew I followed through on my commitments and that I am a team player. This seemed like one more good reason to walk away.

I was telling them I wasn't coming back *because I was not coming back*. I meant it.

After eleven seasons, I no longer felt it was a good fit with my brand or for the direction I wanted to take my business and philanthropic efforts. I was starting to become aware of my young daughter's opinion of the show. "Trashy," she said to me when I asked her. That wasn't acceptable. Any real fan of the show, who has watched it from the beginning, knows I am right—the show has declined over the years. I don't think the participants are paid enough to do what they have to do—become ever more scandalous—to maintain viewership. If I was going to do television, it had to be a platform that didn't sap my energy. It would have to enable me to have conversations with women about entrepreneurship, brand building, and leadership. Any future TV project I was involved in would have to talk about the strength,

> You have to make an exit to make an entrance.

confidence, and innate power that women have. I was intentional about that. The *Housewives* was not the place for me to have those conversations.

I knew what I was walking away from. The sale of my entire Bethenny and Skinnygirl business, which I am currently working on, could have tied into the show in some way. But you sacrifice in the short term for long-term gains. Kevin Huvane, one of the leaders of the Creative Artists Agency (CAA), had given me good advice the second time I left the show, which is worth thinking about in terms of where you are in a journey. "You can never go back there. You have to move forward. You are a person who inspires women so you can't return to that brand." He told me to be gracious, which of course I would be.

I am extremely grateful for the show and what it did for me and my brand. I know where I came from, I know what made me, and I honor the time I spent on the show; I respect it. I am grateful to my fans. After a total of eleven years, now it represents, for me, a moment in time that has passed. I had to be clear in my own mind about the reason I was walking away. I kept my cards close to the vest and I didn't tell anybody what I was doing until the time came to walk. When I announced I was leaving, no one believed I was actually going to do it. I was one of the few Housewives who has walked away voluntarily. Others who have left the show have been fired, but Bravo allows them to just say they retired.

This moment was important for my reputation in the business world. I want to maintain a reputation as someone who says what she means and follows through on commitments and promises. Bluffing in any relationship, whether it's with your school board, your boss, colleagues, neighbors, whoever, doesn't give you any leverage or win you any points. It just makes you unbelievable. When I make any decision, my intention is clear to all involved.

I do not believe bluffing gives you any leverage or points in a negotiation. Actually, the opposite is true: it affects your reputation. Just today, in talking about selling my business, my fiancé, Paul, said to me, "You don't want to give a potential buyer any leverage by telling them where you stand on money. You're giving them the power." I disagree. The buyer *is* in a power position, because I want them to buy half of my business. On the other hand, I'm not going to sell it for any less than what I want. I have a realistic number in my head, and I won't sell it for a dollar less than that. That's what it is, so it doesn't matter if they know the number. They need to know where I stand, and they need to know I'm sticking to my position.

The number cannot be thought of on its own either. It's all about the partner, and I'm in charge of choosing the right one. That's where my power lies. Can they build and grow the business? What is their agenda? The company that bought Skinnygirl in 2011 didn't care about it. Rather, it was part of a strategy to entice a big buyer, which it did (Suntory bought Beam for more than $13 billion in 2014). You don't always realize what the other side's goals are. Beam had its own agenda, and they openly admit to not caring about Skinnygirl. I offered to buy it back at a discount because I am the only person who can grow it. They have driven it into the ground. When I sold it, I was at 360,000 cases a year. After the sale it went to 900,000 cases a year, but now it is down to 250,000 cases. I see an opportunity to take it back and find the right partner to build it back bigger together. Transparency in this effort is key for me.

B SMART

Use Your Words!

If you take anything away from this chapter, make it these truths:

1. Be transparent about what you want from any negotiation.
2. Establish your bottom line and stick with it, even if it means walking away from a deal.
3. Trust your gut. Nobody else has your vision, so stick up for what you want.
4. Don't make idle threats. If you say you'll walk if you don't get X, then walk if you don't get X. Otherwise, next time no one will take you seriously.
5. Try to talk to principals—not their lawyers or representatives. Go directly to the decision maker whenever possible.

Direct Is Best

Now I'm going to tell you a fairly complex story about the journey of my podcast, *Just B*. It's an instructive example of how direct communication every step of the way helped me avoid and correct missteps, ensure no one felt I was being duplicitous (even if they weren't always happy with me), and achieve a good deal with the biggest and best podcast network around, iHeart. There was stress involved, because I knew next to nothing about podcasts when I was first approached about doing one. Like so many times in my life, I had to build the rocket while flying it. I was learning while doing, and honesty kept me from going off the rails. Come fly with me!

In early 2020, I was approached by Endeavor Content, a division of the Beverly Hills–based Endeavor talent agency, to host a podcast. This was an unexpected opportunity that piqued my curiosity. What little I did know about podcasts (next to nothing) told me that this could be a great way to expand my brand, talk about issues that were important to me, give me a creative outlet for personal expression, and allow me to have meaningful but entertaining conversations with amazing people—at a home studio, in my pajamas. Andy Cohen and Paul both encouraged me, saying I would be a natural. Yes, please!

My wheels were turning. The podcast wouldn't be about pop culture, celebrity gossip, or nonsense; I wanted to hear from people who made it to help other people. I would want to focus on people who personified the idea of "mogul" because they made a difference, started something new, or were trailblazers in one way or another. Exciting!

The first call I made after I hung up with Endeavor was to my partners at MGM, with whom I had a development deal, and the head of MGM Television, mostly because I was in the habit of sharing everything I was doing. I was transparent, especially in the beginning of our relationship. I told them a lot, because when I partner with someone I feel that I should be open. This is where some people confuse my niceness with weakness. I explained the conversation I had had with Endeavor—podcasts were not on MGM's radar at that time, so MGM was not yet in that business. I went on my merry way and worked with Endeavor Content to create *Just B*. It launched in late September 2020. I was so busy imagining the show I wasn't paying too much attention to the contract negotiations, which in some ways was a stroke of luck—but more on that later.

If I was going to do a podcast, I wanted to come out of the gate fast and bold. Each broadcast begins with what I call my rant, where I talk about what's on my mind, what's bothering me, what puzzles me or amuses me, everything from online dating to Gwyneth Paltrow's vagina-scented candle to parenting. *Just B* blew up! The show gained serious traction among listeners as well as in the business and media communities. And I was able to secure some incredible early guests.

Shortly after we launched, I received an email from MGM informing me that I had an exclusive deal with them, which prohibited me from doing a podcast outside of our contract. Hmmm... I wasn't sure if this was the case. After all, I had informed MGM about the podcast, and I had been given the green light. I was under the distinct impression that MGM thought podcasts were small potatoes and not worth the effort. They don't actually feel that way today, and the success of my program is in great part responsible for their change of heart.

I called my lawyer, and she told me that the language in my agreement with MGM didn't prohibit me from working with

Endeavor Content, because I was hosting the show, not producing it. This was a crucial distinction. If I had been named a producer on the show, then yes, MGM would have had a legitimate argument. However, my role on *Just B* was to do an opening monologue and then interview a guest. Of course, I had to prepare what I was going to say, and I had some input into who would appear on the podcast. But as star (and not a producer), I didn't owe MGM anything because my deal with the company explicitly said that I could host shows, just not produce them with another company.

Still, the success of the podcast—it reached the top five quickly after its debut—made MGM nervous: Why weren't they making any money off this slice of my pie? My lawyers continued to tell me that I was covered, but honestly, the fact that MGM was unhappy didn't feel right to me. I was upset. I had been such a good partner, and so up front with MGM about everything on my plate. MGM was not in the podcast space at that time, and they did not see it as lucrative. But when my podcast did well, MGM's antenna went up. I didn't quite know how to handle the situation, because even though I had been up front about the podcast from the beginning, I didn't like that MGM thought I had put something over on them, because I hadn't. I shared how I was feeling with a colleague, and she said, Bethenny, this isn't the *Housewives*. Meaning I could not get emotional, and I didn't have to tell MGM everything I was involved with. That's when my thinking shifted. That's how I took my situation with MGM from personal and feelings to just business. I didn't have to tell them everything I was doing; that was not an obligation.

Meanwhile, I still had not signed a contract with Endeavor and therefore hadn't been paid yet. Nothing about the financial arrangement had been clearly defined. It all felt off to me. The only way to turn that feeling around would be to continue to be honest and clear about the situation as it progressed.

This isn't terribly unusual in the media business—you often start work on a project before all the details in a contract are hammered out. The money Endeavor was offering seemed quite low in terms of the work I was doing and the high-profile guests that were eager to be on my podcast. I was reaching a desirable and lucrative demographic as well: young professional women, affluent, employed, college educated. All of that had to be worth more than Endeavor was offering.

The way the advertising was being sold also bothered me. I had recorded an ad for a hair loss product, and saw that it might run during my Hillary Clinton interview. It felt inappropriate to the caliber of my guest and the audience she would attract. There was no discernment—the same ads were being placed in my podcasts regardless of whether I was talking to Hillary Clinton, Paris Hilton, or Mark Cuban. The sales team wasn't seeking out specific advertisers for individual shows; I felt a different strategy could result in more revenue and better advertisers. Even though I knew next to nothing about podcasts, I understood that if you have high-end guests, you should tailor the advertising so the ads are relevant. The pricing structure was odd as well—an ad during the Hillary Clinton program would cost the same as an ad that ran during an interview with a lesser-known name. This didn't make sense to me.

While I was still hosting shows, we went back to the table and asked Endeavor for an amount of money that we felt was reasonable and in line with the work I was doing. It was not a crazy amount, and anything less would not be worth my time. Endeavor pushed back and offered me an embarrassingly low figure. It was a number that would make it difficult for me to justify the time required for the podcast. Maybe I was wrong. I had to gain more knowledge about the world of podcasts and advertising; otherwise I couldn't go back to the table with confidence and clarity. If I was going to stand my ground I had to have solid footing. Instead of telling Endeavor I was walking away, I stepped back and called people who I knew were doing successful podcasts, including Dave Portnoy, who founded Barstool Sports, and actor Michael Rapaport.

Dave told me that my podcast, because of the nature of the guests, should do custom selling versus bulk selling. Light bulb! That's why I was seeing hair loss ads scheduled for all my podcasts! They were bulk-selling ads instead of pursuing a "matchmaking" strategy of pairing the right advertisers with each podcast subject and guest. Dave said that if we had confirmed Hillary Clinton, then that particular show should be pitched individually to specific advertisers who would be willing to pay a premium to be on that specific program. Ditto for Mark Cuban and all the other guests. So my initial instincts about advertising were right. This was one important piece of information.

Michael Rapaport provided another piece of the puzzle. He explained that there were two ways to do a podcast: fifty-two shows that run continuously for a year, or fewer shows, say thirty, that are also broadcast weekly, after which the show goes on hiatus for several weeks. Then it's relaunched as a new season. At the time I didn't want to do a series that I would have to relaunch; it seemed like starting from scratch on something I had already developed into a brand.

After talking to additional podcasters, I realized that Endeavor was fairly small in the podcast world, and for that reason not as powerful. That may have been part of the reason for the low money they were offering me and its bulk ad sales strategy—lack of clout in the space. All of the information I had gathered was valuable in terms of how I would approach Endeavor, who was not just producing the show, they were airing it as well, acting as a de facto network.

Ultimately, it was clear that we couldn't make a deal with Endeavor. It wasn't just the money, but the ad sales strategy and the size of audience we could reach. I decided to leave the table and find another production team. The important issue was not shutting down the store while we moved into a new one. Listeners shouldn't notice that we had changed locations. I called MGM, who had by this time come to terms with my arrangement with Endeavor. Once again, I was up front about my thinking and suggested that they consider producing the show. I also told them that I would be calling iHeartRadio, Spotify, Dave Portnoy's company, and others in the podcast space.

iHeart is the leader in podcasts, so I especially wanted to talk to them. I wanted my work to be with the best, because I knew it would be a success. I knew what I wanted to say to iHeart, but whom should I call? I didn't know anybody on the executive team, but I had met someone on a dating app who worked at iHeart. I sent him a text and asked if he knew anyone in the podcast division. "Yeah," he texted back. "I know the person who runs it."

I googled the name my dating app guy sent me, and there he was: Conal Byrne, then president of iHeartPodcast Network, the most powerful person in the podcast industry. Okay.

I had his number, and on Halloween weekend 2020, a Saturday night, I cold-called him. He answered. I introduced myself, explained the circumstances of my call, and asked him if he'd be interested in making a deal. He's smart: he knew the number of listeners my podcast was reaching. The show was on his radar.

"Absolutely," Conal said. "I absolutely want to make a deal, but do you have to worry about Endeavor?" I told him I didn't have a signed contract. He explained that iHeart had a relationship with Endeavor, and perhaps iHeart could help with the agreement. I put iHeart in touch with my business manager to worry about the money. It turned out to be the most up-front negotiation I had ever been involved with. Conal is honest, straightforward, and transparent. When we moved to the contract stage, if we got stuck, we'd get on the phone and talk it through. He would tell me where he could not budge, and I believed him because he was telling the truth.

I knew from my long experience with *Housewives* negotiations and other deals that when you enter a space where you are unproven, you don't make as much money until after you've built traction. In this case, I had been in a weird purgatory with Endeavor during which I had shown that my podcast was successful. I had strong proof that I could deliver to iHeart. I know I was not a Joe-Rogan-hundreds-of-millions-of-dollars kind of fish, but I was a real fish in a major pond. It was a happy accident that I went through this little dress rehearsal with Endeavor without a contract, and without making any money.

Now I went back to MGM. They were still feeling stung about my podcast. They were still annoyed that I wasn't doing the podcast with them, so I said I could give their newly formed podcast division some street credibility. "I'm happy to have you guys produce it, and it will put you on the map by associating you with a successful podcast." MGM's response was that they'd have to figure out what was going on legally, in terms of our contract. My reaction was, what do you mean? We're clear on this, I don't have an obligation to host a podcast with you. I was frustrated. I am a loyal partner, and I didn't like the way I felt. It was not going to be a good partnership.

We went back and forth about it, and our discussions put a bad taste in my mouth about them and in their mouths about me. I felt shackled. At this point, I had to decide where the podcast was going. I had developed *The Big Shot with Bethenny* for TV with MGM as the producer. I also had a deal with MGM that said any programming I wanted to produce had to go through them, including podcasts. I also knew that deal was coming up for renewal. MGM was essentially telling me that if I didn't play ball and do the podcast with them, they might not want to renew my contract.

That was good information, because I didn't want to renew my contract with MGM after all of this. Any renewal would lock me in. Yes, they would have to pay me a great deal of money, but the price of exclusivity seemed too high to me. I was envisioning the big picture, the end zone, the field goal, and the touchdown. There was no guarantee I'd be better off if I pulled the trigger and said, I'm going to leave. But I also knew there was a tremendous chance that big things would come as a result of being free of them. It was worth the risk, even though I knew that if I stayed I would be getting what was essentially free money every year from MGM just to produce my ideas through them.

The deal would have been too constricting for what I thought could be huge creative and financial opportunities in the future. I wanted to be free to work with whomever I wanted to work with. I don't like to be told who I can and can't work with and what I can or can't do. I want to be a free agent. And I had to tell MGM that—and it was not something I was going to tell their lawyers, because lawyers are a go-between. I wanted to go directly to the source so there would be no misinterpretation of what I was saying.

I called the head of MGM, and I said, "I don't think you should renew me. I don't feel like I'm going to be a great partner because I'm not going to play by the rules, and you want me to. We have a difference of opinion, let's just launch this one show." Whew. Yes, it was hard, but how else could I have handled it? This was the right way, as it turned out, because we ended up parting on amicable terms.

We launched a successful show on HBO Max. The mega-streaming service took *The Big Shot* because of me; MGM had never ever sold a show to HBO Max before. Likewise, MGM did me a solid because they have the power and the strength as a platinum-level production company, along with having Mark Burnett and his expertise. I remain good friends with Mark Burnett to this day.

So what about the podcast? Endeavor wasn't thrilled that we were only using them to produce the show, not to stream it. I was worried that if Endeavor had the podcast, how would I make sure that I owned the library of programs and that the transition would be smooth? I don't worry about the dollar; I worry about good sense. I told my then business manager to think beyond the money transferring from Endeavor to iHeart, which I now had a deal with. That issue became a big rub in our negotiations. We had to stop and relaunch the show as a new product—something I thought I did not want, but that turned out to be a happy accident. Relaunching meant all new public relations, marketing, photos, and a new media announcement about my deal with iHeart.

It just goes to show that the things that I, as a layperson new to podcasting, was worried about were the exact things that ended up becoming important when I was finalizing my deal. Trust me, the things you're worried about *do* matter. No one's ever going to think of things the way you do. The squeaky wheel does not always get the oil, meaning you just can't bark about everything all the time. However, when you're trying to work out a deal you have to speak up and ask the questions that are on your mind. We were trying to transfer over from Endeavor to iHeart. I wanted to get the party started. The situation was sensitive because iHeart works with Endeavor on other deals. But who owned my library of shows? Wouldn't that be me? Let's move this deal along and pay me what I'm owed.

We were moving in circles on this issue. I kept quiet and observed. Finally, when the numbers of circles that were being run around got to be too many, I picked up the phone. I was on a call with the business affairs people representing Endeavor, but the deciders and dealmakers from Endeavor weren't on the call, even though they were supposed to be. The woman I was speaking with said she would give a message to Endeavor. Since the people from Endeavor were not on the call, I had to make sure the message I was giving to the go-between, the legal team, was clear and concise. I didn't want it to be misinterpreted. I did not want to be misquoted.

Okay. I said, "Pass this message along: I want to date other people. I'm sleeping with other people. I've gotten engaged. I'm breaking up with you. I want to move on. My next phone call is going to be Ari Emanuel or Patrick Whitesell." Ari and Patrick run the parent company of Endeavor. I've known both men for many years, and I would not call them over something trivial. I continued, "Please allow us to break up now, because the reason I left you guys in the first place is because of this jerking around. So now, it's no longer funny. This will get less funny and more public quickly so please facilitate the breakup immediately, because I'm moving and I'm dating. I'm now married to iHeart. That's the message." I did not lose my temper, even though I was angry. I was firm, controlled, and clear.

I'm not going to tell you that this was a fun conversation. But when you are sure of what you want it's also not difficult to say it. Not long after, my business manager called to tell me that Endeavor was letting me go completely; they were not going to produce the podcast, and I was now a free agent. Yahoo! Next up was getting paid for all those successful shows I created. Once in a while somebody has to get slapped.

This is a perfect example of when things get sticky or unclear, if you figure out exactly what you want, how you want to do it, and communicate it clearly, you will win.

Go to the Source

If something is bothering you and you feel stuck emailing back and forth or texting about it, stop. Get on the phone with the source. Be friendly and confident. Compliment them, and then explain what the problem is, and ask how it can be worked out. I would never have been able to do the Beam deal for Skinnygirl had I allowed lawyers to go back and forth in an endless stream of nonsense "on my behalf." When Beam reached out to my business managers to say they were interested in acquiring Skinnygirl margarita, I didn't want to leave everything up to lawyers. This was my brand, which I had created, and it was a part of my identity and my overall business vision of creating products that solve problems. It was my baby. I also knew both the product itself and the name had tremendous value in the marketplace. I was not going to leave it up to others to work out the details for me. I got on the phone with the president of this multi-billion-dollar company and said, "This is what I need, let's meet in the middle. We're rational people, let's figure it out."

The same is true of any arrangement you're trying to work out. Don't screw around. Don't play games, and don't get caught up on the little things. That's how deals get blown up all the time, whether it's buying and selling a house, accepting a job, or going into business with someone. People underestimate the leverage they have, and as a consequence, they are afraid to use their words and ask for what they want. If you have to, write down what you want to say before you say it. Think it through and let it marinate overnight or over a weekend. Rehearse with a friend, so when you make the call, you're confident you can pull it off without becoming emotional.

It does take courage to stand up and be clear, but the payoff is so amazing. Courage is a muscle you can build. Challenge yourself just once to say what you mean and mean what you say. You will realize you're still standing, as is the person you just talked to. The next time will be easier, and it gets easier every time. You still have to prepare, you still need to know what you want and can or cannot compromise over, you still have to keep yourself in check, but it all gets more natural and organic.

You Have to Be Able to Handle the Truth

I live and die by my word and my actions. If I make a mistake, I admit it. I don't tell lies to make people feel better or myself look better. Transparency and honesty are in my DNA. I owe a big part of my success to that.

Saying what you mean, the truth, lives on a two-way street—you have to be honest with others, and you have *got* to be honest with yourself. Can you handle the truth: delivering it and receiving it? If not, start working on it. Once you start to succeed, the game begins moving quickly. Honesty is my default button and my protector; it's helped me navigate many treacherous waters.

Fame is an interesting thing in the context of honesty, and it applies to everyone. That's because there are varying degrees of fame. The only difference between my fame and your fame is in the amount of recognition we each have. You might be known in your office or in your town or your family. Just remember that you want to be well known for being good at what you do, and not for being a jerk. When you become relevant, you're a target. The truth will set you free.

When I started on *The Real Housewives of New York*, I was not well known. My stint on *The Apprentice: Martha Stewart* didn't make me a household name. Still, I was not going to be someone I wasn't on the *Housewives*. It was not an opportunity for me to become another person, it was me being me becoming famous (for lack of a better word). It was a process, like any other life process— like the first year of marriage, becoming a mother, or the first year of building a new business.

The only way I could even hope to leverage what I was doing into a career was to be honest about who I was, which was someone who was trying to launch a business. There was no way I was going to be on a television show and pretend that I was born with cameras outside my house, or that I had more than I did. I was dead broke that first season on the *Housewives*, and I was paid a pittance—less than $7,300 for the entire first season. That was next to nothing for work that was grueling, invasive, and emotional. I went through the experience of becoming famous in real time on that show. Learning, becoming, evolving.

Honesty and transparency are also crucial if you're the first person in an arena. I was the first person to seriously and publicly monetize reality television, and that exposed me to all sorts of scrutiny, doubters, and criticism. My Skinnygirl margarita made me a pioneer in creating a new low-cal cocktail category. I changed the cocktail industry. Everybody was watching—there was no room for bullshit around that product. I knew what I wanted, which was to keep all the financial interest related to any business I was involved in during the show—and I was up front about that. It was an integral part of the new contract negotiation. Before I came along, if you were on a reality show, you had to give a percentage of what you earned from any business you promoted on a show to its network. I never did that, and it became known as the Bethenny Clause, which was a disruptive moment. People were paying attention to how I handled contract negotiations with the show because I had businesses aside from reality TV that I was building. When people sign a contract with a reality show these days, you better believe they ask for the Bethenny Clause.

I talk more about these kinds of business strategies in other chapters of this book. My point here is when you're drawing a new road map and writing history, you better be real, because everyone is watching. False moves are noted and remembered. Don't get cocky. Be authentic and up front.

There was a woman on the *Housewives* who was fired, and she was honest about it. I thought that was admirable, not just because she was being honest about something difficult and potentially embarrassing, but because her honesty could help other people in a similar situation comes to terms with losing a job. Some people bullshit everyone when they get fired, or they have some false narrative about what happened. That doesn't help anyone. The same thing happens around plastic surgery. People have it done and then pretend they didn't when it's as obvious as the nose on their face. Lying or pretending nothing has changed and everything is perfect does not help other women, it damages your personal reputation and integrity, and it diminishes their self-worth.

On the *Housewives*, and even today in all my projects, it was and is important for me to communicate to women how to get the things you want in your life, and how challenging it can be. I just cannot do that without being honest with my audience, and with myself, about who I am. Likewise, whatever you are famous for, express it through honesty. If you get caught being disingenuous, it hurts.

B SMART

Discretion Is the Better Part of Valor

Being honest and transparent does not mean spilling your guts or revealing private matters to the public 24/7. It may not seem as if I am a private person, but I am and always have been. There are big buckets or categories I keep private, like my daughter, how I feel about things, how I process information, plans and strategies that I have yet to execute, romantic breakups, and so on. The fact that a relationship didn't work out may not be private, because that information easily becomes public (and if you are a public figure, you often do have to announce events like splits, marriages, pregnancies, job changes, and so on, before the gossip columnists get to it). However, the reasons a relationship didn't work out are personal and no one's business. Yes, I have opened up publicly about many aspects of my life, and I can be vulnerable. If that can benefit somebody else, I'm all in. But they don't need to know all the details to be inspired and helped. The details are private.

There are other times when you need to retreat, which is an honest thing to do. Not long ago, I said to myself, things aren't going so well. It was a feeling I had because in the real world, everything was going great. It was not as if I was being negative; I simply felt like the wolves were at the end of the bed, sitting and waiting to pounce on any vulnerability. It was one of those times when things might look like they're going too well. The table *will* go cold—if it hasn't happened in a while, expect it will happen

---

soon. That's how real life goes. Those are the times when you want to go with your gut, keep to yourself, and lay low for a while. There's nothing dishonest about pulling back; it's self-care and self-preservation.

Keep yourself honest and keep yourself humble—sounds simple enough. Except that it can be extremely challenging in today's climate. It is difficult not to show people how great everything is all the time, especially on social media. Social media is the devil because it enables a lot of false bragging, and entices you to show off your fake "best life." We are living in a period of enormous focus on "look at me" as in "look how good I am at this job or this dance," or "look how great I look in this pair of jeans or this dress." "Look at how amazing my eyelashes are," and "look how pretty my long hair is," and on and on. People are on the other side of that, feeling bad about themselves. The electronic visual world we live in has added a dimension of narcissism to our lives that isn't healthy. The pressure to always show the happy face and the perfect outfit and the perfect children is driving us mad. It also makes us dishonest because the pictures we present of our lives force us to continually prove everything is beautiful all the time. And that's just not reality.

The reverse side of the pursuit for digital perfection is that people are quick to tear everyone and everything down behind the safety of their smartphones. I don't like any of it, because the truth is, I spend 95 percent of my time in pajamas, with my hair in a bun, my glasses on, reading and writing and planning. When I have pictures taken and I post something, there's this push to make it perfect. I don't like the fact that I sometimes feel like I'm pretending that everything is perfect in my world, and it's not. I love my life. I work hard. I laugh, have fun, and enjoy my blessings—but I don't always look glamorous doing it.

I don't want to post perfect pictures all the time. I don't want to look like I just walked off a movie set or a fashion shoot, because I didn't. That's not how I live. If I post a photo of myself with makeup I always try to give credit to the person who did my makeup and am obvious about having my makeup done professionally. No one lives that way, and I don't want to pretend otherwise. This fake perfection is an illusion that makes other people feel bad about themselves. It drives people to depression and worse. That's why I post photos where I'm not in makeup; I'm in sweats or a T-shirt and jeans giving business advice or cooking tips. I sometimes look at the results and think, *God, that's what I look like?* Yes. That's what I look like. While others are faking their lives, keep yours real.

Honesty in your personal life is one bucket. Honesty in business is another, and it is so crucial. No one wants to do business with a faker. My brand is me, and my integrity is on the line with every piece of clothing, sunnies, or food product or home good I sell. That's me the customer is buying. I am also honest with partners and colleagues, even though it can be hard. It's easier to avoid confrontation and difficult talks, but you're just postponing the inevitable.

Several years ago, I attended two different parties; I met Kevin Huvane at both of them. The first time I didn't know exactly who he was, so I think I said something like, hello, and I think we know some people in common. Then I asked him what he did. He told me he was a managing partner of the Creative Artists Agency. The second time we met, we again chatted, and he shared that he had shepherded the careers of some of the biggest actors in Hollywood including Meryl Streep, Sandra Bullock, and Sarah Jessica Parker. The top guy. Oh, okay.

After the second meeting, I cold-called him, and told him that I had many different things going on—reality television, product development, other business ventures—and many deals were in the works. Would CAA represent me? The answer was yes. I worked with Kevin and CAA for several years. The agency was able to help me get great branding deals. At one point in my career, I decided that I didn't want or need an agent. I called Kevin and I said I was leaving the agency world. I was not going to someone else. No one was on the back burner. I wanted to try to do it on my own. He's not the type of guy that you leave. He's never kept in touch with or kept a relationship with the people who have left the agency. Instead of doing what everybody else does, which is lie and then run to another agent, I said to him, this isn't working for these reasons. I could be wrong, but I want to do this part of my business on my own. I just have this feeling I should do this on my own. I'm not going to another agent. And I wasn't and didn't.

He wasn't thrilled, but he was fine with it. I'm not saying the conversation with Kevin wasn't difficult, because it was. We didn't speak for a while, not in a bad way, or because of any animosity. It just happened that way. We did keep in touch when it was appropriate, and we are close friends today. I can still talk to him, and he's one of my business confidants. We respect each other. He is a good agent who has built a lot of important careers, so the appearance of disloyalty hurts. Agents are human too.

I believe that how you walk into something and how you walk out of it should be the same every time. It should be honest, forthright, and dignified. The same is true when one of my assistants or other employees wants to leave or when I have to let someone go for whatever reason. I always make them feel safe. I don't run to clear out their desks and escort them off the premises. I am sure there are human resources people who disagree with that, but I want people to feel safe and happy. It's not that deep. I always want to take care of the other person.

Honesty helped me when I was shooting *The Big Shot with Bethenny*. I talk about some of the struggles and challenges we overcame in shooting in other chapters. Part of the story demonstrates so clearly why being up front, and not confrontational, but vulnerable and compassionate, wins the day. I didn't love the original casting on the show, and the way the show was being shot didn't feel right to me. I talked to my producer about potentially recasting the show, which was a big deal. It would have been costly in time and money to send people home and find new people. We also had concerns over safety and security around the pandemic. I felt I had to open the lines of communication, because I felt as if I was having these secrets in my mind, and that was so unhealthy. It wasn't right. The game was moving too fast. I wanted an intimate show. The crew seemed doubtful. I felt I was in over my head.

I had another producer working with me, and I kept asking him, is this okay, is this shoot working? And he kept reassuring me that it would be all good. He didn't tell me the truth, but I had a gut feeling. He didn't lie, exactly; he just was not honest and was trying to keep moving forward and make me feel better. I had to dig to find the truth because no one would tell me. You have to go with your gut. What was worse was that *no one* wanted to tell me what was going on: that the crew didn't feel good about how it was going either. It was a disaster that everyone was pretending didn't exist.

I had to collect myself and talk to the executive producer, Jaimie Glasson, and tell her, we have to put on our big girl pants and make changes. But. And there was a but. I had to address the cast and crew. That was on me.

I was absolutely a leader. That was my obligation. I knew the temperature of the room. It was cold and weird, so this speech I was about to make wasn't going to be easy. The show felt wrong, everyone knew it, but no one wanted to say it.

The next day, I gathered everyone together and said out loud what they were probably all thinking. "Most of you don't know me. You may think I'm some reality show clown that's coming in here thinking she can produce a television show because she was successful on some other train wreck show. But I am a business person. I care about my brand, and what is happening here is not who I am. I would rather not do a show than do something that looks and feels like this. This will never happen again. Going forward we will have an honest and open line of communication."

I told the crew that I knew the show was a disaster, and that I was going to do everything I could to pull it together. People need to be led by somebody who's telling them that they understand what's going on, and they look into your eyes and understand your language when you say it. That's when we all feel safe together. That's the point. I talked to them from the bottom of my heart. I told them that going forward we were going to do things differently. I ended up getting the respect of the crew that day. That little speech cracked everyone wide open. It was like a mass sigh of relief went through the room. I could feel it. Honesty got us through to the other side. And then we made some much-needed changes and created what I think is a great show.

5

Stay Five Steps Ahead

TO BE SUCCESSFUL IN BUSINESS, WHETHER AS AN ENTREPRENEUR
or in corporate America, you have to be fiercely aware of what is
happening around you and understand what it means for you.
True moguls (and yes, you can be the mogul of your own life,
and you should be) look at the whole chessboard while also being
aware of all of the pieces, and put what they see together so they
can stay five steps ahead. This is the way I think, and I believe it's a
strategy that can be learned by paying attention and making strategic connections between events and/or cultural shifts. You have to
train yourself to think this way; to look, see, and think about the
relevance to what's going on around you.

Part of training yourself to be aware comes from being intentional, which I've already discussed in detail. It involves looking at
the big picture, all the potential players in an event or decision and
what impact they could have on your decisions, and all other factors (economic, social, cultural, etc.) that are involved or could be

affected by whatever decision you make. More than that, you have to be aware of global factors that can affect your life or business.

One example of how looking at the big picture can be an advantage, one that is always relevant, is the real estate market, something I am personally interested in. The value of real estate and how it changed during the course of the pandemic is particularly instructive. When cities were just starting to shut down, in part because urban areas were being identified as hot zones for the spread of COVID, I saw friends in the city looking to get out. Those who were fortunate enough to have weekend places outside of the city left to stay in those homes. It didn't matter if they had school-age children—learning was virtual and could be done from anywhere. Those who did not have a place looked for rentals.

I noticed this movement and predicted that even more people would want to leave New York and other cities, many for good because the future seemed uncertain. Many of these people would want to buy in the suburbs or even farther out, in rural areas. Before the selling and buying rush started, I thought it would be a good idea to act quickly and buy a place outside of the city, before inventory became tight and prices skyrocketed. I was right. That is what I did. In fact, I bought and renovated and flipped several houses in Connecticut during the pandemic. So not only do you have to learn to think five steps ahead, you have to be willing to act on what you see.

I am always tuned in to the culture. Not just in real estate, but in fashion, food, and other areas of interest to me and my businesses and philanthropy. That means I am connected to my fans and followers. I have a gut instinct about what bothers them and what problems they need solved. Most of the things they care about, I care about too. I'm a mother, so I know and care about the challenges my daughter and other girls and young women face. This helps me see relevant issues, create solutions around them, and comment on them. All of my product lines solve problems and fill needs that I feel are not being served well in the market. I believe this is one of the reasons my podcast is so popular and why it struck a chord with listeners right out of the gate.

Aside from amazing guests, I do a short rant at the beginning of each program, where I talk about social and cultural issues that are personal to me but that I also know other people are thinking about—from gender pronouns to online dating to plastic surgery to dieting. Listeners connect to those rants and enjoy them because I touch on topics that most people think about but avoid talking about publicly. I mention it all! In fact, my rants are popular. The most frequent listener comments indicate that my rant is the most popular aspect of my podcast. As an experiment, I started doing some all-rant episodes (no guests) to see if the fans would come and listen, and they did! Millions of downloads came as a result. The rant is the reason why I was popular on the *Housewives*. I provided the Greek chorus, the running commentary on what was happening. The venting, the humor, the satire—I love it, and the listeners love it too. I asked iHeart how I could do a second show, one that would let me rant every day. I can record months worth of rants in advance that can be aired every day, and twice a week I will do an interview. Two shows, two different models. Both amazing.

We all need to see beyond the moment we're in while still living in the present. You have to be checking boxes and plugging holes at all times. It's maddening, of course, but the fact is, it's essential. More annoying: being good at business will often not be good for your well-being, because the more you become obsessed with and attentive to the details, the more details there are to attend to, and the less time you have to take care of yourself. It feels good when you've stopped a gap, but there are always new chasms to fill.

B SMART

Think...Ahead

Seeing the big picture takes practice, but as with any other muscle, you can work it and improve your skills. I want to mention a small detail that was the direct result of seeing five steps ahead and what significance it can have for your success. I was the person who thought to trademark the name *The Big Shot with Bethenny*. Yes, even big companies with huge staffs like HBO, Warner Brothers, Bravo, Amazon, Walmart, and MGM are not always on top of everything. Details can get lost. We were already well into working on the reality series when the production studio realized they hadn't registered the name. This affected the timing of the announcement. We had to hold back on it because, technically, we didn't own the name. I said not to worry, I've already done it—which gave me some leverage because I now own the name, simply because I was the only one thinking about making sure it was registered.

This reminds me of another similar story that happened years ago. One night I was watching a television program called *Diners, Drive-Ins and Dives*. Looking at all the crazy food, the oozing cheese, truffle oil, and giant sandwiches, I thought, what I'm looking at is food porn. Hmmm...one day I'd like to do a show called *Food Porn*. The next day, I started working on getting the name registered. Don't assume anyone is smarter than you, a concept from my book *A Place of Yes*. I called an intellectual property lawyer, who completed the legal work for me. Not long after, I owned the name Food Porn. Surprisingly, it was not taken, so I was able to snag it.

Lo and behold, an agent (now producer), who, coincidentally, years before had refused to represent me even after I begged him to, called my team to say that he had tried to register the name Food Porn and was blocked because someone named Bethenny Frankel got there first. He was shocked, thinking, why the heck does Bethenny Frankel own this name? He explained that his company had sold a show with the same name to a network without bothering to check to see if it was already taken. "We want to give you a credit on the show in exchange for the name," he said. "Nope," I replied. "You're going to compensate me financially for using it." And they did. Every time the show aired I was paid a lucrative producer fee. I did nothing but register a clever and valuable name, because I was thinking—and acting—ahead.

I'll Drink to That . . . Maybe

Not long ago I was approached by a company about creating a rosé wine. This call got me thinking about the wine space, especially because my noncompete agreement with Beam had expired. I was now free to enter the spirits world again. I called the partner who had worked with me on Skinnygirl margarita to talk about the idea and the winery involved, and specifically to see if he would be interested in working on the product's development with me. Interestingly, he told me that he already had a rosé wine that was bottled, packaged, approved, and on shelves, but it was experiencing low sales. This was a different scenario than years before, when I had to go through the laborious and complex process of creating my own label for Skinnygirl margaritas and getting it approved. That can take a long time. My former liquor business partner further explained that there were two small internet influencers involved in the marketing and branding of his wine but that its sales were still slow.

I liked both the name of the wine and the product itself, which is imperative. I don't slap my name or endorsement on just anything. It has to be good; it has to be something that has value and quality, and that is aligned with my brand and my values. I said I would work with him as we did with Skinnygirl margarita but only if the two other people were out of the deal. I also said that I would include the wine in *The Big Shot with Bethenny*, which would certainly give the brand a boost and raise its profile. I never waste media real estate.

The premise of *The Big Shot with Bethenny* was competition-based but outside of the format of shows like *The Apprentice*, which I feel is no longer relevant. The intention of the show was to be an authentic search for someone to be an executive on my team, who could take the reins of some aspects of my business and become my eyes and ears. It's a tough job, and I sincerely wanted to use the series to identify a great person.

The contestants met several challenges and worked on actual business projects. In that sense, there was nothing fake about the show. There would of course be a finale, when the winner of the competition was announced. The event would also include a party and celebration that would be filmed as part of the show, which coincided with my fiftieth birthday. Including a branded wine in that event made sense.

As we continued to work out the details of the deal, we also started shooting the reality series. I even had a dress to match the wine for the event: a confection of frothy pink feathers that was so pretty and perfect for promoting a rosé wine.

The beautiful party was filmed with my partner's wine displayed as a backdrop. It had to be done this way, even though I had not signed a contract for the partnership—the timing of the show demanded we work the product into it while we continued hammering out the contract. Had we not, we would have missed an amazing television opportunity to promote the wine. Meanwhile, I had also registered the name of this wine in other categories. My partner only worked in the spirits arena and was not interested in branching out. The name of the wine was only registered or trademarked in spirits. There had been numerous opportunities for him to register the name in a variety of categories outside of spirits, but he didn't. I did. Five steps ahead.

Everything was coming together for a great launch of a delicious wine. The promotion of the wine in this way was similar to the time that I wrapped my car in the Skinnygirl logo and used it on the *Housewives* to make one of my entrances. As I told one of my *Housewives* colleagues, who was sort of poking fun at me for making my car into a commercial, if you can wear an Hermès belt, or anything with an obvious logo, on television, I can drive a car wrapped in a logo. It might as well be my own. "But, darling," she said, "they aren't paying me." I looked at her and said, "Exactly. That's the point." Why would you do a big brand's advertising for free? Why not use any opportunity you have to advertise your own brand?

I was excited to be in the spirits business again, especially given the timing of my new show. These kinds of opportunities are important to exploit in every way possible because television offers a chance to tell a story. When you can create a compelling narrative around a product, that product becomes more accessible and relatable to potential customers. Entrepreneurs know to look for opportunities to tell those stories. The reason that I've been able to execute these unusual marketing ideas in ways that no one else on television has done is because I see many steps ahead. I literally created this model, and look how many celebrities have followed suit.

The partner asked me why I had registered the name of the wine in many other product categories. I told him that if we were going to do a deal, I would want to use the name for other products—and that I would give him 15 percent of everything earned from any categories that were brought to market. He had had two years to register the name but hadn't. He said he would not do the deal with me if I didn't give him the intellectual property, the name, I had registered. This is where the deal got held up: he said he wouldn't let me use the name in other categories. He wanted to focus on spirits.

At this point the wine had already been filmed on the show, but the deal was about to fall through. I was not going to give up the intellectual property rights to the name in other categories.

I was upset because the wine had now been incorporated into the show. We needed to plug this hole. I am as deliberate as possible, even when things are moving quickly. There are also times in life and work when you have to take a risk and play fast and loose. You can only do this well if you are five steps ahead and working out future scenarios in your mind. I knew that I didn't want to let airtime go to waste, so I had to find a way to make the show work, even without this wine. I called HBO Max and the production company to explain the wine situation. In this case there was a solution. We ended up blurring the name of the wine bottles and cutting some scenes, but ultimately, while it wasn't ideal, it did work out but it was subpar.

Soon after that wine deal fell through, another wine company's executives approached me about another opportunity. I have known both men for many years, and I was interested in what they had to say. It was a similar story to the one my old partner had told: they had produced an excellent product; it was named, bottled, and on the shelves, but it had low recognition and sales. The wine company, Forever Young, started with a delicious rosé. In fact, the wine was better than the previous one, more elevated, and produced in the south of France. Forever Young also didn't mind if

I registered the name in other categories, for the same 15 percent. They know the lane they're in.

It was fortunate that the product was available too. There is no point in promoting something people can't buy right when they are thinking about it. I see products marketed too early, before consumer availability, because there is enthusiasm and excitement to tell people about them. The problem is, nobody cares about "coming soon"; people care about right now. When you capture someone's attention, you better be able to put that ball into the basket.

> **Don't overplay your hand.**

Shut It Down

At a certain point there was a chance I wouldn't be able to share this wine story in the same way because I came close to shutting down *The Big Shot with Bethenny*, and had I not been thinking five steps ahead, I would have. *The Big Shot with Bethenny* is based on an idea I had for a show I called *The Successor* that would take viewers through my process of finding my company number two. As I mentioned, it came from my true need for a right-hand person. I called producer Mark Burnett to tell him about this and a couple of other ideas months before we ended up deciding to do a deal. Mark had bet on me because at the time I was the nobody and he was somebody. I called him after serendipitously running into him at a *Shark Tank* press event. It was one example of the crazy full circle of me being a contestant on *The Apprentice* years ago and then having the balls to call Mark Burnett! At any rate, I told him about the different shows I wanted to do, and he liked *The Successor*, which was ultimately renamed *The Big Shot*.

The idea and concept for the show went through a number of processes. The production team and MGM were amazing at knowing where to pitch it, who's buying what, and ultimately selling it to HBO Max. They are excellent at what they do, and I want to give credit where credit's due. During the press experience, I explained that this was my show and my baby and if it fails it's me, and if it wins, it's me, but I also have incredible partners. The show didn't fail or succeed: it did well, people tuned in, and it enabled a conversation with viewers. When it came time to talk about renewing, I brought what I learned about myself and my business to the table. I didn't like mixing my real business with television. Having a production team and cameras around stops you from running a real business. My business is too serious now to expose it to something that injects a different kind of energy into the mix.

But let's go back in time a little further. I was walking on the beach in Los Angeles right before we were about to sell the show. I wanted to reconnect with longtime reality television producer Jen O'Connell, who is now executive vice president of nonfiction and children's and family programming at HBO Max. I first met Jen when she was running Ricochet, the production company of *The Real Housewives of New York City*. As I took my walk, I texted her and said, "Hey, I'm in LA, would you like to get a drink?" I hadn't spoken to her in years, but Jen is someone I respect. We met and talked. Long story short, she made the decision to buy the show from me for HBO Max.

Keeping in touch with people and connecting, being credible, and saying what you mean, meaning what you say is also staying five steps ahead. Jen doesn't like everything I've done or said. We've definitely argued, especially on the *Housewives*. But I've always had integrity, I've always been levelheaded, and I've always been someone who's going to deliver. She has integrity too. We respect each other.

Once we were rolling, there were the inevitable COVID-related delays, and what seemed like millions of contract hiccups. Despite the usual issues, we were off to the races. We started in the same way that *The Apprentice* started, by sequestering cast members in a hotel. We also had the best in the business working on this show, from the camera people to the director. The production values were on an elevated level compared to other reality TV I've been involved with.

We started shooting the series at my house in Connecticut. I knew it would be jarring to have so many people roaming around a space I hadn't even moved into yet—the house seemed too small and the crew too big. But there were *so* many people, crew, staff, assistants, food service…and on and on, as if we were shooting a Coca-Cola commercial. On the day filming began, the people who were being sequestered in the hotel, our applicants, were also going to join everyone else at the house. It was a zoo! There were coffee rings all over my counters; the house was a wreck. I went up to the front door of my house when they had already started shooting, and I fumbled with my keys. I couldn't even get into my own house. They were shooting the contestants, and I said no, you have to get this, this is real life! I want to show real. I am not good at being in a formatted show, I am good at being me. This is not a corporate show about corporate enterprise; this is about working in my world. And sometimes you can't get in the front door! Let's do real!

It was so important for everyone to understand this was not going to be a typical reality show about hiring a corporate employee who will work in the corner office on top of a skyscraper in Manhattan. The show is ultimately about me living through what's truthfully happening in real time. The production people had told me to be ready three hours before they needed me, and I was wondering why they weren't upstairs filming me waiting during all the craziness of that—because that's the world my number two person would be stepping into. Why weren't we capturing the important parts of the show's story and my story—my flaws, my rants. We were missing out on a lot of valuable content, content that would differentiate us from every other similar show and that was truthful in terms of who I am. We were in between two worlds and two shows.

As I realized what was missing, I was worried and wondered why there was not one camera upstairs in my room capturing the minutiae of who I am, and capturing an important part of the show's story, and my story. The way the show was being shot felt corporate, weird, and uncomfortable. The executive producer, who has worked for years on major formatted shows, didn't understand what I was trying to do. It took hours, days, and weeks of me saying, no, you have to understand, like, this is where the fish are—in the minutia or everyday life, the fish are not feeding on the big moments. It's about the small moments.

The production crew had wanted to put a microphone in my ear and tell me what to say. No. This train is moving too fast and it's going off the tracks. I didn't want to do it that way. I couldn't get hold of it. It felt wrong and disorganized.

We had heard that we had to shoot the first episode in one day because of all the money they'd spent. That meant we were shooting until four o'clock in the morning on Election Day, and my birthday. I looked over to the two main producers, whom I liked. We had talented producers working on the show. I was also looking at the clock and worried. I asked the producers if it was legal for the cast and crew to work these long hours. I thought it was unheard of. I've never seen a more disorganized production, and that wasn't what I wanted.

The producers said it wasn't a union shoot. It's not illegal but it's not right.

My only thought was that I had to get these people out of my house and into their own. We had to shop shooting. It felt so wrong in so many ways. It also happened to be an unseasonably cold day in November, maybe 30 degrees. I was outside shivering with frost coming out of my mouth. Everyone was freezing, and as a consequence they were rushing even more frantically. My gut was telling me that this wasn't going to result in a quality show. It was not turning out to be what I had envisioned *at all*. I had to think about making an unpopular decision, to pull the show.

I called my partners, MGM, I called my business manager, and I called my lawyer. In the back of my mind I thought, *Oh, they're going to think that Bethenny is being a pain in the ass diva,* but it was wrong, and I had to make the calls. I said to them, "Who do I talk to? Do I call HBO Max?" That's like calling the principal, that's the network, and they all said to me, No, no, no. Don't do that to your partner. But I sold it to my friend Jen, who has known me for years. She didn't buy the show because of MGM. She bought the show because of Bethenny Frankel. My name is on the show. People would tune in to see me. It would all be on me if it failed—no one would care about MGM, no one is going to blame Mark Burnett or the producers. It was my name that was on the line.

I called Kevin Huvane, the head of CAA, who remains a friend, and I asked him, *What would you do?* He said, of course you should call Jen. When I did, my frustrations spilled out all at once. "Jen, this is a disaster. I don't think we have it. I know it's COVID and I know it's stressful and I know it's an election. But I don't think we've got this, okay. We have people sequestered at a hotel for weeks, away from their kids, missing Thanksgiving with their families. I don't think we've got this. I know this is costing millions of dollars so I get why no one wants to tell you about this. But you know me. I've never called you. I don't take this lightly. This is a disaster. In my entire career I've never seen anything like this." I was willing to give it up.

Jen responded in a way that made me feel much calmer. "We're not walking away from the show. We have you, this is a big show for us. It's important to us. If we have to shoot it later, we'll shoot it later. We're not like a conventional network; we don't have to be on time for a specific season. You're our secret weapon." Her words made me feel good, reassured. I felt safe, but thinking about it also made me feel sick, because we were shutting down the show. I told her to give me a couple of days.

I pulled myself together, took the lead, and called the producer. I said to her, "Listen, you have one day to decide if we can do this show. You're a successful woman, you've worked in television for years. This show is important for both of us, and it's important for women. It's you and me, baby. We need to get through one day. Can you get through one shooting day? Can you do that?" She didn't answer me right away. Instead, she said, "Let me get back to you." The next day she called and said, "I think we can do it." Yes. I knew that if we could get through one day successfully, we could build on that accomplishment. It would give the producer, the cast, and the crew the confidence to keep moving forward.

We walked into the shoot a couple of days later. Right before the cameras started to roll, I pulled the whole crew together. These are people who are top in their professions—a major director and a major photography person—and I'm sure they were thinking I was some loser reality star. The rule is, you get the best of the best if you want to have the best product. You can have the greatest car, but if you have a clown driving it, it's going to crash. So we had the best of the best, but no one was driving—no one was thinking five steps ahead. Tensions were high. The crew all deserve a round of applause. They did nothing wrong, but the game was moving too fast during a difficult and stressful time—a pandemic! I had to collect myself, open my mouth, and take the wheel. And that's exactly what happened.

I said to them, "That first night was terrible. But listen to me. That was a shit show. Most of you don't know me. That is not who I am. But I can promise you that it will never happen again. That is not the culture I want. That was not the show we are doing. That is not what I set out to do. It's not me, it's not HBO, and it is not Mark Burnett. I know it's a pandemic, it is an election, it is a stressful time. I understand. Listen to me. All we have to do is one day right. Just trust me. One day."

We did that one day, and it was a success. The rest of the show went smoothly. It gives me chills thinking about it. At the end, everyone said they were proud to have worked on the show and that we had turned a difficult situation around. It was what I wanted it to be: spontaneous, unpredictable, and unformatted. I did what I felt in my gut. But I also scared the shit out of everybody including HBO Max because they didn't know how it would all ultimately go down. They didn't know why I was doing what I was doing as they were watching the filming from the feed. They were thinking, hmmm… we didn't know she was going do that. Everyone who was used to following rules were disconcerted by the filming. But it was all okay, because it was coming right from my gut. It was truthful and not manufactured, packaged TV show bullshit.

> You can have the greatest car, but if you have a clown driving it, it's going to crash.

The Big Picture Is Made Up of Small Details

I always say I sweat the small stuff. I see the big picture and implications of the small things that I know could have a big impact later on. I spend most of my life remembering details. I try to say hello to people and remember who they are, even though I'm not good at names, because you never know what connection can be helpful later on. I am a homebody and an introvert, but I still like and respect many people. No one gets back to people more quickly than I do, because I understand everyone's time is valuable, and I want to nurture and maintain contacts. It's almost not fair to hold people to my standard, but I do.

Not paying attention or being blind to the consequences of small actions can often hold up progress. Likewise, understanding that small things can have big consequences is huge. I've had staff who did not pay bills on time on my behalf, which in turn has held up house renovations. If something doesn't get done this week because we have not paid a lawyer or contractor on time, something else has to be delayed, and it's a domino effect. Pretty soon the renovation timeline can be off a week, and then a month, and then six months. Expenses and material costs increase, and you could be in the hole. You have to be ahead of the game, at every level.

Of course you should not focus on the small stuff that doesn't matter. And there are things I would push for the next time, but you never want to push people too far. Don't overplay your hand. I know where the line is. I see the picture, so next time I'll ask for a different credit if there is another season of the show, or a different financial arrangement. I'll decide. I play the long game.

See everything. More than that, put it together, see how the pieces fit and find the meaning: see the potential and the pitfalls. This is how you stay five steps ahead.

6

Know When to Hold Them and Know When to Fold Them

THERE IS A TIME TO LOOK FOR A NEW JOB AND LEAVE AN OLD one, end a relationship or begin one, sell a house or buy one, learn something new or refine and update an existing skill. There is the right time to make changes in a business, and a time to hold off until conditions in your industry or infrastructure change. There is also a time for sitting still and a time for movement. When you are undecided about your next move, that's when you need to sit still. Timing is everything when it comes to pivoting. How do you know when to make the right decisions at the right time? I'm good at timing decisions; I have a gut instinct for it. But I also believe people can attune themselves to timing, to knowing when they should make a move, hold, or fold.

Oftentimes we let ourselves get too deep into what excites (or worries) us about our business or life, and we can't see the forest from the trees. We can become emotional about business ideas, or too wrapped up and attached to an idea in a way that makes us inflexible and unable to think clearly about what is best for us. Facts get in the way of our fantasy, and that's not good. In terms of business (and relationships too!), this passion or emotion prevents us from looking at the big picture. We miss important details, such as how competitive our product or idea will be in the marketplace. We miss warning signs to slow down, like shifts in trends or fashions, changes in the economy, or new competitors on the horizon. Overthinking things can also make us stuck. If you take the emotion out of your thinking and look around you, ask questions, read the news, put the pieces together, you will develop a good instinct for making decisions based on the truth of your situation.

Bottom line: think about reality and not just the daydream. But stay in touch with your gut. Are conditions right in the market for the idea? What problem is it solving, and is there a great need for that problem to be solved? Remember too that the best ideas are often the simplest. Think about Uber, Facebook, eBay, Amazon. All basic concepts that solved common problems: getting from one place to another; staying in touch with people and groups; finding collectibles that are unavailable locally; and buying anything you need without leaving your couch. The Skinnygirl margarita was successful out of the gate because it was so simple: a low-cal cocktail. In fact, it solved two problems that were not being addressed in the alcohol market when I launched it in 2009. First, it wasn't sugary, which meant that women (primarily) didn't have to worry about enjoying a drink or two at happy hour after work with friends, or at a cocktail party. Second, Skinnygirl margarita is ready to drink, meaning no mixing or measuring. It is good to go straight from the bottle. Convenient! Ready-to-drink cocktails were not a big segment of the spirits market when I created the cocktail, but I knew women (underserved in the market) would respond to something that was delicious, low-sugar, and easy to serve.

When we brought the product to market, it was just one flavor. Still, it was popular because of the exposure it received from the *Housewives* and my own press. It was the one brand I had executed essentially on my own, and it has been the most successful by far. As the brand grew in popularity, I had to think about whether I could produce enough of it and control its quality on my own. Many brands have stumbled because of this. In 2017, the direct sales company LuLaRoe began receiving numerous customer and salesperson complaints, and eventually lawsuits, about its popular leggings. They had gone from high quality to being poorly sewn from substandard fabric, and would arrive to customers damaged and ripped. The company had started to cut corners when demand increased. I didn't want something like that to happen with Skinnygirl. A sale to Beam not only represented a financial deal I could not say no to, but it also meant being bought by a company with high standards that would maintain the quality of the product even as the market for it expanded. It wasn't just that: I needed muscle behind the brand for it to succeed, and in this case that meant the power of robust distribution by experts in the industry.

There are other questions you have to ask yourself about your business. Do you want to stay small or create a national presence? Many people want their businesses to remain local or highly curated, like the successful farm stands and seasonal produce markets I see in the Hamptons. Would you like to build a brand that could be sold to a larger company? Do you want to own 100 percent of your business versus owning a smaller portion of it, which could give you the opportunity to earn more money or enable you to have a greater impact? You could also be shackled by a partnership, or stymied, so you have to consider that as well. With Beam, I didn't know when I made the deal that years later they would tell me the business was not important to them, even though it still makes money. They have bigger fish to fry.

You have to forget your ego when you answer questions like these. A pivot based on ego or your emotional attachment will be a bad one, whether it's around a business decision, charity, a relationship question, or a parenting dilemma. Think objectively.

As I often do when I am considering a major pivot or change, I talk to trusted and experienced business people. I make my own decisions, but I value the advice and perspective of those who have walked the path before me.

Suzanne Somers shared this wisdom with me. "All negatives are opportunities. It's how you respond to the problems that defines you." When she was fired from *Three's Company* for having the audacity to ask for more money—since she was a huge audience draw—she was devastated. She was ostracized in the industry and shunned by former colleagues and friends. Shortly after being let go, she was walking down Rodeo Drive in Los Angeles, and she said, "The wardrobe guy who worked out the look [for my character Chrissy] saw me and turned the other way and crossed the street."

What did she do? She took some time—almost a year, in fact—and then reinvented herself. She realized that "everybody in this country knew my name," and that recognition had value. Soon she was starring in a Las Vegas production with thirteen dancers and a twenty-seven-piece orchestra, performing a revue that included pop standards. In 1987, she was named Las Vegas Entertainer of the Year along with Frank Sinatra! She also went on to develop and market one of the most recognized and successful, not to mention iconic, pieces of exercise equipment in the world: the ThighMaster.

It just goes to show you that you cannot be defined by the failures and the disappointments in life. You have to leverage them for what they can teach you, and appreciate them for the new directions that they show you.

Supermodel and super mogul Kathy Ireland also shared her thoughts about pivots with me, and it was fascinating. A little background: Kathy runs one of the largest and most successful licensing companies in the world—that's right. In 2019, Kathy Ireland Worldwide was number 26 on the list of Top 150 Global Licensors. She also made the first *Forbes* list of America's most successful self-made women in 2015. Her multi-billion-dollar business, which now includes clothes and home furnishings, real estate, hemp products, insurance, and substance-abuse recovery and rehabilitation centers, is an incredible story of growth, determination, and pivots. And this major business started with a line of socks she produced in 1993, which sold more than 100 million pairs.

Kathy told me that becoming a model at age sixteen set her up to accept rejection with grace, pivot, try again, and never give up. "I was underestimated," she said, as the businesses and people she was reaching out to thought of her as just a pretty face, or worse, a "dumb model." Kelly Ripa and Suzanne Somers have told me the same thing. "But there is power in being underestimated," Kathy said. "You can use it to your advantage."

Be Sensitive to Cultural and Social Shifts

When faced with any decision about change, you first have to think about the result you want—and that can be in your business, your relationships, or your personal life. You have to look around and observe what is happening in your profession or market, and what's happening in your community, region, and the world. How might current conditions affect the outcome of any move you make? When you see trends in the culture, insurance, taxes, real estate, politics, or anything important, think about what these trends mean for your life and business. How quickly can you respond to these changes?

When deciding to stay or go, sell or buy, change or remain the same (at least temporarily), think about reality, as I said. It's also important to be nimble in your business.

Kathy Ireland did a smart pivot with her brand Kathy Ireland American Home, which for many years worked almost exclusively with luxury estates and properties. Responding to changing social and economic conditions in the housing market, this division of her company pivoted to include affordable and middle-income rental homes. With her real estate partner, the company is building hundreds of affordable rental properties for middle class and at-risk families using many home furnishing products from her own line of lighting, flooring, and so on.

The pivots I'm thinking about and those that so many other savvy business people consider every day are large-scale versions of taking the temperature in the room. Pay attention! The world gives you so much information if you're willing to put your ear to the ground and listen, and apply what you learn to your situation. For instance, I believe that the evolution in the apparel business and the body positive movement has shifted the relevancy of the word "skinny" as it relates to clothing, except for shapewear, where I believe it remains relevant as a concept and name.

I kept this in mind when I was developing a line of swimwear, which I discuss in depth later. My gut told me that if I were to launch something like a swimwear line, I didn't want to do it under the Skinnygirl name. First of all, Skinnygirl began as a margarita, a product I developed when I was a young woman, and primarily for other young women who were emerging, maturing, and developing into unique adults. When I brought the idea for a swimwear line to HSN, I was thrilled to be met with enthusiasm—but they wanted to keep the branding under the Skinnygirl name. I cannot fault them for that: they wanted to stick with a proven brand. But I had strong doubts about that.

I thought the line, which I defined as elevated, sophisticated, and inclusive, would be better branded under the Bethenny name, a brand I had developed with a more mature businesswoman, mother, entrepreneur, and philanthropist in mind. It was a reflection of where I was in my life. The brand would also reflect my company's evolution. Many of my fans and followers were at this stage in their lives as well. Bethenny would be inclusive of curvy girls and all the beautiful shapes and sizes of womanhood. The timing was right for this kind of branding, and Skinnygirl, as much as I love it, just did not feel right for certain products.

I respect and value my HSN partners, and I felt strongly that Skinnygirl should not be the only brand name for apparel. I knew HSN would give my idea serious thought. My point is when you know the timing is right, others may not see it. You have to persist. Eventually, my HSN partners came around and realized the wisdom of putting swimwear—a challenging and sensitive category for so many women—under the Bethenny umbrella.

It's also not always easy to know whether the timing is right when everyone else is synchronized differently. The retail market is always shifting; trends and interests change. Demographics evolve, and the needs and wants of consumers fluctuate as a result of numerous factors, including the economy, employment and salaries, social mores, and cultural values. You need to become sensitive to what's happening in the culture, and how any changes may affect what you're doing or how you approach your work and take it all into consideration.

B SMART

Bake It In

Timing the right decision is like baking. All the ingredients are laid out in front of you in the right measures. You put them together in a certain order to get the result you want. It's the same with timing a decision. You need to gather all the information (your ingredients), weigh them and measure them in terms of importance (quantity and quality), and put them together to make a whole in the right order (follow instructions).

(Real) Estate Planning

One of my great passions is real estate investing, specifically buying and renovating homes, adding to their value, and flipping them. Because of my interest in real estate, I've learned a great deal about it and have become aware of and sensitive to shifts in real estate markets. For example, two days before the 2016 Trump election, I had found an apartment in Manhattan that seemed to be grossly underpriced, given its size: more than 4,000 square feet. During the run-up to that election I saw how emotional and passionate people had become about the candidates. Many people in New York, and I am sure in many other places, were unsure of what would happen if Donald Trump was elected. The real estate market was in temporary paralysis—which to me meant it was a good time to buy. When everyone is stopped, you should be moving.

When I found the apartment online, it was listed as a three-bedroom, so anyone looking for a four- or five-bedroom, appropriate for that square footage, would not see it in their search results. You had to dig and search by size, not by number of rooms. The photographs were also poorly done. I think many buyers had probably passed it over for these reasons. I could see it was a diamond in the rough, and in a location I wanted. I don't play games, so I put in a full-price offer. Today, as I write this, I could get much more than what I paid if I were to sell it because I bought it at the right time.

Likewise, when the COVID pandemic first started in early 2020, I had already talked to Paul about my interest in getting a place in Connecticut. The chance to spend time in the suburbs was appealing. I loved going out to the Hamptons where we could have a real backyard and green spaces, but it was a couple of hours from Manhattan on the best day—and in heavy weekend traffic, getting out there can be a nightmare. Connecticut seemed like a great alternative, with many appealing towns only an hour from the city. Months before COVID became a public health crisis, as I discussed earlier, my gut instinct told me that Connecticut would be a good place to buy a weekend house, close enough to Manhattan to commute during the week if we decided to extend our time away from our home base in Manhattan. The towns we were looking at also had the right vibe for a family.

Some areas of the state had seen dramatic boom times, especially during the 1990s and early 2000s when many New Yorkers moved to places like Greenwich and Westport because of their proximity to New York, great school systems, and some tax benefits. During that period, the city was holding less allure for many people. These factors combined had made some Connecticut real estate super expensive. By the mid-2000s, the scenario had changed. The city had become more appealing again—it was safe and booming. People had started to move back in.

Several months prior to the pandemic, prices in Connecticut towns within commuting distance to New York were lower than they had been in the past. I learned this because Paul and I were at a birthday party in mid-2019, where I met one of the principals of a major real estate firm. I told him that I was interested in looking for a house in Connecticut, and he mentioned that it was possible to buy a property for up to 40 percent off the usual prices because the market was soft in part because the cool factor of Connecticut for Manhattanites had diminished. I don't care about cool for myself; I only care about what works for me and my family. I thought that was a crazy interesting piece of information, so I tucked it away in the back of my mind. We weren't quite ready to move...but I wanted to be prepared to do it right when we were.

Then COVID hit. During the early stages of the pandemic, many people were frozen in place, not sure what was going on. I didn't know how the pandemic would play out either, but as I explained in the previous chapter, I am always thinking five steps ahead. I was looking at the chess board, and the pieces. People had to get their lives sorted out. Even in a not great market, one of the opportunities I saw was that people in a rush to get out of the city would want something turnkey, a house they could move into and start living in. Most people don't want to do renovations, especially during a pandemic. That was another potential upside I saw—if I was willing to do some work, and I was, I might be able to get a great deal. I was in a position to do so if I did see a deal. I never put myself in a situation where I am trapped financially. I can always act if and when I need to.

Schools were also starting to shut down, ostensibly for a couple of weeks to "flatten the curve." At that point I was thinking more about a house in Connecticut, and I had also started to consider changing my daughter's school, not to one in Connecticut, but to a good school in Manhattan. My gut told me that while everyone else was paralyzed and stocking up on groceries and paper towels, no one would be thinking about applying to private schools in New York.

The timing seemed right to get Bryn into a school with a tough admissions policy. Schools might be worried about enrollment dropping and tuition fees disappearing. Why not at least try to get her enrolled in one of the amazing schools in New York, one that is normally nearly impossible to get into, while there are so many other things happening that are weighing on people's minds and distracting them?

Even though she wasn't that far into her time in fourth grade, the fall would come quickly. I thought, do it now, while no one was looking and before everyone else started scrambling. I learned this philosophy from relief work—you need to act fast and be a first responder if you want to be effective and help mitigate chaos before it takes hold of a situation. The fastest and most nimble people win the day.

I called the school, and it turned out my instinct about enrollment was correct: it was a surprisingly pleasant process. Success: my daughter would finish grade school in what is arguably one of the hardest schools to get into in New York. Some people might say it happened because of who I am, but that is absolutely not true. There are many people in Manhattan with far more recognition, power, and money than I have who can't get into schools like this. Many private schools do not like the potential circus that is attached to well-known, high-profile people. However, I was no longer on the *Housewives,* so there was not a circus around me. In many ways, I had retreated as a media personality and had evolved into the role of working mother.

Once I decide I want to look for something, I *scour* and dive deep. That's how I became an expert on certain topics, like real estate. Ask me anything about real estate in the Hamptons, Connecticut, and lower Manhattan. My feeling was it didn't matter if I was ready to buy or not, it was the right time to put a stake in the ground in Connecticut. Sometimes you have to jump to fly. It was a gut feeling, but it was also based on what I was seeing around me. I had recently watched a television show about wildfires in California, and one of the main characters kept repeating that "motion is life" as in you have to be moving to live. It was a metaphor that resonated with me at that time. I wanted to move on a house in Connecticut, if not into one. I started looking at houses.

I also realized that most people can't pivot on a dime when it comes to real estate and moving. They would have to sell their place or at least rent it out, find a place to buy, and then move—and many people during COVID weren't thinking that far ahead. I had a pretty strong feeling that once things settled down and more people realized what was going on around them in terms of the social and cultural side effects of the pandemic, the suburbs would blow up.

Many things in the world started to change in surprising ways. Low and slow quality cooking and upscale local seasonal luxury food from farms became popular. That to me was an indication that nesting and staying home would cause a cultural shift away from eating out in the city every night. The supply chain was starting to fracture. Luxury watches, outdoor clothing, and even boats and cars were becoming difficult to find, and they were in high demand. Again, this told me people were looking for comfort, quality, and ways to spend time outdoors and with their families.

Cities were about to decline. People were going to start moving out of the city. In fact, there were some months in mid to late 2020 when you could not find street parking to save your life in many residential neighborhoods in Manhattan, from the Upper West Side to the East Village, because so many moving trucks were lining the streets. This isn't an exaggeration. New York remained a ghost town for many months during the pandemic, even as street crime continued to rise.

Obviously, nothing's truly cheap in New York–accessible Connecticut towns. Some of the houses I looked at needed work, which would add to the ultimate cost of the property—but at least I wasn't looking at crazy multi-million-dollar fixer-uppers. My plan was to find something nice and charming as a part-time place. With the help of a real estate agent, I found a home I could renovate and flip, as well as a second home that I could live in, which could become a retreat. Both homes were on the smaller side, but both were more than livable. This strategy may not work for everyone, but when I buy an investment property, it has to be something I would live in if I had to. That way I know that if I am in a situation that necessitates it, I could be happy in any property I own.

I moved, and while the first house I moved into didn't end up suiting my needs, I learned that I absolutely loved Connecticut. However, the house was not big enough to accommodate everything I had going on with my business and employees. The second house I bought could easily become a weekend retreat, however, because even though it was smaller than the first, it was set on many more acres. It was nestled in a beautiful setting. I knew I had two good houses in a great market. I renovated both of them. I admit to chasing the dragon on the first house, in terms of renovations. I should have

Sometimes you have to jump to fly.

done everything right from the beginning, and ended up throwing good money after bad. Still, I didn't lose money on the purchase. But I did learn a lesson: do it right the first time.

I'd taken some profit off the table in the first house in terms of the renovation choices I made, which were personal to me and not necessarily valuable to a general buyer. For instance, I had installed an outdoor shower, which probably didn't add a great deal of financial value to the property but it was something I wanted.

Even so, I would make a multiple seven-figure profit on both houses when I sold them. That's right, we sold both houses while the market was still growing during the long months of pandemic anxiety. The people who bought the first house love it, which makes me feel good. They were the first to look at it, and shortly afterward, they extended a decent offer, close to the asking price. When I get a serious offer like that, I don't play any games. I always say pigs get fat and hogs get slaughtered, meaning that the person who holds out and is greedy can get killed in the process, because they don't react to timing correctly; they let their emotions get in the way. I do not fuck around that way. The first offer is the best. It's been proven time and again.

Even better, the people who bought the second house also bought all of the furniture. It wasn't a huge additional sum for all of the furnishings in a large home. However, to me the purchase represented the value of convenience. When you sell a house and no one buys the furniture in it, which you may no longer want or need, you have to deal with getting rid of it somehow. You either have to keep it and store it, or sell it off individually or at an auction. None of those options are time savers. For me, the fact that the buyers made an offer for the furniture was beautiful. Time is money. Yes, please!

Both were good houses in what became a phenomenal market (a good house in a bad market would sit for a year, maybe more). We timed the sales correctly. Maybe I could have held out for more money, but the buyers were right, and I didn't want to be emotional about these sales. I didn't want to be the hog that got slaughtered. And I didn't want houses I was not planning to live in to be nagging at me, pulling my attention away from other, more important things. I don't ever want to be jammed up or stuck with things I no longer need.

It can be challenging, but please try to take the emotions out of real estate or any other kind of commodity or business transaction or decision. If you don't, you can miss out, because emotions interfere with timing. And remember, no one ever went broke making a profit.

> Pigs get fat and hogs get slaughtered.

Watch Yourself

Another unlikely example of learning when to hold them and when to fold them comes from my passion for watch collecting. I've collected fine watches since I was thirteen years old, when a family friend gave me my first luxury timepiece as a gift. I was fascinated and intrigued by this beautiful watch, and it ignited an interest in me that stands to this day. I was hooked! I went on to become a serious collector, even during a time when luxury and vintage watches weren't trendy or cool in popular culture. I am also unusual in the watch collecting world—traditionally women have not been collectors in this area; serious watches are not marketed to women in the same way they are marketed to men. As a consequence, I taught myself about watches by looking at them and studying the market. Over time, I developed a sense of what was good, even if it was a watch that wasn't wildly popular or sought after at the time. Many watches I own may not be the hottest or most fashionable watch when I buy them, but I know enough about the market to recognize a superior timepiece that will grow in value. As a result, all of my watches are major. I have an excellent watch collection, and I would say that 75 percent of my watches have doubled or tripled in value.

The luxury watch market, like any market, is constantly changing. It is a commodity, like luxury handbags, fine jewelry, and sports cars. Tastes change and evolve. There are watches that I could have bought, and should have bought, that would now be worth triple the price I would have paid. Then there are watches that I own that, while I like them, I don't feel passionately in love with them, nor do I wear them often. I assess these watches from time to time, no pun intended, in terms of selling. Is it right to let them go? If it is, I sell them. I'm not emotionally attached to them. If I was, I could not make rational, strategic decisions about buying and selling. I also do not trade out of high-end watches that I bought at retail because that is considered a no-no in the watch world. I only sell watches that I have acquired on the secondary market.

There are certain watches that you can't even touch at certain times because everyone wants them, and that demand is reflected in high prices. There is a watch pro I often use to help me buy and sell watches when I am ready to let one go. One day not long ago, I asked him about investing in a certain watch, but since the watch market was experiencing a level of high demand, I was uncertain whether I should make the purchase. When any market is hot, whether it is watches, real estate, or any commodity, it is better to be a seller rather than a buyer. You may not want to do both at the same time either, because you could end up just breaking even. However, you *could* buy something that you feel is going to go up in value *if* you see something that no one else sees. It's nuanced, yes, and you have to understand the current market.

That was the situation I found myself in. For instance, I own a rare, large, green-dial model 116508 Rolex Daytona. It had become popular but not yet achieved cult status. I go with what I love even as an investment. I spend money, I don't waste it. It's a spectacular watch. In the watch world of 2020, it was starting to be discussed—and worn. It was being seen and photographed on the wrists of celebrities like comedian and actor Jonah Hill and singer songwriter John Mayer. There was a years-long wait list for the watch, and it had finally achieved cult status. And I had one. It's now worth 50 percent more than what I paid for it.

My next watch obsession was with the blue-faced, white-gold Rolex Daytona. Few watch collectors were looking at it, but I loved it. I wanted to get my money into that watch and get out of some of the other watches I had. I spoke to my watch dealer about selling some of my other watches so I could get into that one. It was good timing, because in this case I saw that the market was good for many of the watches I owned but wasn't attached to, and not as good for the watch I wanted. Sometimes, depending on what you are buying and selling, even in a strong market, a pivot can make sense. He helped me find the right buyers for some of my watches, and I purchased the blue-dial Daytona. I feel confident about these transactions and feel I made a great investment.

Don't throw good money after bad.

Stay or Go?

As I write this, I am seriously thinking about whether I want to take on a financial partner or an investor into my business. Mark Cuban said to me, "Why do you need the money from an investor? You don't need it. What will you do with the money?" His advice was to keep the business ownership as it is and not bring in an investor. My fiancé, Paul, has said the same thing to me: "You don't need the money." But I do need the added value, meaning I could use a partner who knows how to grow my business in smart ways and has the leverage to make strategic growth happen. For me this pivot would not be primarily about the money. It's about getting the time to do other things that I could gain by having someone take over the management responsibility for many aspects of my business. It's about the ability to expand into areas that I cannot easily manage to be in as a solo owner.

Right now, like many business owners large and small, I have to deal with the infrastructure, the hiring, people management, finances, and office space. I need a strong team of internal and external people, employees and advisors. If someone else could help manage my infrastructure, that would be a pivot that makes sense to me. In your business, think about whether an outside party could help you financially, with growth and strategic planning, legal matters, or whatever box you need checked that you cannot check off yourself. These are big questions for me because now that I am fifty, I think about my health, motherhood, time, and quality of life. These are hugely important concerns as I weigh the pros and cons of selling a stake in my brand.

Other people have said to me that whoever you partner with will eventually become someone whom you have to answer to. As a person who likes to be on her own, I find this is a valid concern. However, I also feel that if I can find the right partner, one who can handle the day-to-day operations of the business, I would be free to innovate. The challenge is finding the person who understands and can work with the personal nature of my business; so much of the success of my products is based on the customers' relationship with me and my role as the face of the brands.

I'm thinking especially of my brand Skinnygirl, which has been around for more than a decade. How do I know if Skinnygirl will become iconic over the long run? Can it go the whole distance, and become another Newman's Own or Amy's or Ben & Jerry's? Do I have what it takes to make that happen on my own? Does the brand have the staying power to become a classic? I own 100 percent of my business, and it has no debt. That is serious equity. I could ride it as a solo act and not be able to take it to the next level. It's also possible that I could ride it to the bottom by myself, without strategic help.

When you build a brand to a certain point, whether or not to sell it always becomes a conversation. I have already decided that I don't always want to work at the level and pace I am working at now. That doesn't necessarily mean I will sell everything. It means I may work differently and approach the business differently. But how? What's good for me, the brand, and the business? Should I sell everything and focus on my podcast? Should I sell the brand but stay involved in its product development? I'm thinking through those questions and taking the temperature in the room, looking around and learning. Any decision I make has to be timed properly based on what is happening in the market, in the world, and in my life.

If I do decide to sell, I will be selling something that has measurable value. My brands have integrity and quality, the products are high quality, the business makes a profit, and it has no debt. I own it 100 percent. There is no one to deal with but me, which makes for an attractive offering. I also know the company could be much bigger, and I am not sure I'm in the position on my own to make it what it could be. I am not a mass-market manufacturer or retailer. This will be one big hold-them-or-fold-them, so it has to be done right.

It's a lot to put together, and I can't do it without help. Yes, I am alone in my decisions (we'll talk about that later), and I will be the final decision maker when it comes to the future direction of my company. But that does not mean I'm not going to seek information to make the best decision at the right time.

I proactively asked Paul to help me figure out how and what I should do—hold it or fold it—and when. We're now on a listening tour. I will continue to seek out and talk to a broad swath of people, including those who have expressed interest in buying the brand and those who have not. We're gathering insights and opinions. We listen, learn, and then make our own recipe.

One of the people we talked to works in private equity, making capital investments into companies that are not publicly traded. The first thing this person told me was that I needed a thought partner, meaning somebody who's going to help me make a decision at the right time. Could that person help me take my company into the end zone, or is it another company that comes in with money and they put a CEO in place, or do they just buy it and take it over? There are so many ways to take a company in a new direction, and there is a time to do it—but it has to be the right time.

"Thought partner" is a great phrase and concept. I would rather people tell me what they don't know, so then I know what I need to learn. I don't want to deal with monsters in the dark; I need to see them in the light of day. If everybody's acting like they know what's going on, we're going to get lost, we're going to lose time, and we'll make bad decisions—and there is never a right time for a bad decision.

My point is, there's no shame in my game. To this day all of the wonderful advisors I've spoken to have been great with advice, perspective, and insight. Each of those people has suggested I call someone else. I take it all in, call the next person, and on the search for information goes. We're calling everyone and anyone in the arena who is willing to talk to us. We will listen and learn so we can make the right decision at the right time.

I also know that when I talk to this vast array of people, they also realize that I work harder than anyone, and I have street cred. Most of them feel confident about investing in what I am doing because they know they're not investing in popcorn, or shapewear, or coffee syrup. They are investing in the jockey on the horse. That's me, because my brands were envisioned by me, created by me, and have evolved because I am completely invested in them.

Anyone can do their own listening tour, scaled to the size of their business. I also did an internet search of the companies that buy brands, celebrity brands, and lifestyle brands and called them. That's something anyone can do, and most of the time you will get a call back. Not everyone will be a good partner or offer the right advice. Be kind, say thank you, stay in touch (you never know), and keep moving. I am a big fan of crowdsourcing. Gather all of the information, put it together, and make your own pie. And then, and only then, decide what to do.

As you continue your journey, remember, don't let grass grow under your feet. Keep moving, because moving is life. Know the timing of things by looking around, listening, and seeking information. Then and only then will you know when to hold them and when to fold them. It's an ongoing journey.

7

You're Only as Good as Your Weakest Link

IT'S ABSOLUTELY TRUE THAT NO ONE WILL EVER WORK HARDER than you on your business, no one will care about your business the way you do, and no one will ever express your vision and passion for it like you will. However, if you want to grow your business, or expand and evolve your brand, at some point in your entrepreneurial trajectory, it will no longer be feasible for you to do everything required to grow on your own; that's bad business. You have to be on top of everything to be successful, of course, but you will have to get out of the weeds and focus on big-picture evolution.

By "in the weeds" I mean getting pulled into day-to-day details and minutiae that are a waste of your time, because someone else on your team or in your family can handle it. For example, I don't need to okay the kind of camera being used when we make a Tik-Tok video; there is no need for me to attend every production meeting before I do an HSN appearance; nor do I have to physically oversee every detail related to maintaining my house. Yes, I do sweat the small stuff and it is hard not to get pulled in, but I have to work on not letting that happen on every minor facet of my life.

You have to be militant about not getting caught in the weeds if you want to grow. You need to get in and out as quickly as possible. The other essential? Building the best and strongest team you possibly can. When I first started developing my brand Skinnygirl, I needed help. In the beginning, I hired young women who were full of energy and enthusiasm, but who didn't have a lot of business acumen. As my business and products have grown and expanded, I have had to look for a different kind of help—people with business experience in areas that I didn't necessarily have, who could help me expand and grow strategically. I still needed energetic assistants, but I also needed people with experience to strengthen and lengthen what was becoming a much larger chain. You need people with different skill sets.

This knowledge creates a dilemma for entrepreneurs who are passionate about their business and want more from it, but have a visceral, personal attachment to it. Even if you're not micromanaging the business, you have to stay connected to it, and there will be times, as I said, when you will get pulled back into some of the weeds. Having a business is a lot like parenting. You have to pay much more nurturing attention to a newborn than to a toddler, and you have to pay more physical attention to a toddler than you do to a fourteen-year-old, who needs emotional attention, or an eighteen-year-old, and so on. Of course you continue to care for your child as they grow, but the relationship and their needs evolve and change, and so must you. The balance of needs and your personal involvement is constantly shifting. Business works in the same way: you have to tend to a young business much more closely than you do once it grows and you have systems in place and people who can help you; you can allow them freedom to take ownership of their jobs, and you get the time to innovate.

In my case, I have an emotional and deeply personal connection to my brand Skinnygirl. Although the Skinnygirl logo was designed to embrace all women, it is based on me and associated with me at a certain point in my life. My other brand, Bethenny, is my name! You can't get more personal than that. This fact can make it challenging for me to be dispassionate about the brand, but if I can't see my business clearly and unemotionally, *I* risk becoming the weakest link. I work hard to prevent the emotional impulse by treating the brand like the serious business it is, checking in with myself and my partners when necessary, and looking at the big picture to ensure the business is running smoothly.

Even if you *don't* want to scale a small business into a big one—and small is a valid business model with potential for sustained success—your brand still must stay relevant and remain sensitive and responsive to customers' changing needs and desires. The work required to achieve those goals can't happen if you're stuck in the muck of minutiae.

> **Get out of the weeds and focus on big-picture evolution.**

How to Create Strong Teams

Let it go, as Elsa in *Frozen* sang. I talked about the idea of the ebbs and flows of the life of a business—most new businesses last five years on average. When I interviewed Steve Madden on my podcast, he said that in order to grow you have to let go. Scary! Especially when *you* are the brand and the business. You know so much about what you do and how you do it. It can be hard to articulate everything in your head to the people you bring into your business. That means there's a new learning curve for you and for anyone you hire to help you. There will be serious growing pains. Ouch! Letting go means taking the plunge and creating a team: hire people to help and then delegate to them. Trusting in others takes time, thought, and money. You can let go and create a disaster if delegation is not done properly. One kink in the chain and a link becomes weak. That's why I believe that you are only as good as your weakest links.

Instinctively, entrepreneurs have a tendency to hold on. We worry, obsess, and micromanage. It's in our nature. We sometimes have a hard time with the word "team." I want to feel excited that I have a great team, so I've put together a set of team building strategies that are helpful whether you're hiring part-time help or putting together an entire staff.

Establish clear goals and expectations. This is a powerful and effective way to help people understand the results you need and demonstrably achieve them. Clarity around roles in an organization can also shine a light on whether the person did the job or not, and whether they did it well. If someone doesn't know what they are supposed to be doing, no one is happy. People want to know what their roles and responsibilities are, and clarity gives you, the employer, a way of assessing them and providing guidance and constructive criticism.

Look for hard workers who align with your mission. You have to understand the strengths and weaknesses of each member of your team so that you can delegate well, making sure the right people are owning the right tasks and responsibilities. My filters for employees are loyalty, hard work, dedication, and being a good person. If someone demonstrates those four qualities they are worth my nurturing, training, and investing in their continual improvement. It's a balance: sometimes people can be *too* good at something and they can dangle that value over your head, using it as a bargaining chip, which is the opposite of loyalty. You always need to find the balance. Absolutely, I want my team to grow and evolve, but if someone feels their success gives them unlimited leverage, it may be time to talk to them about finding a more suitable job outside of the company, especially if your business can't accommodate their professional dreams and goals. Most companies do not and cannot offer a "sky's the limit" growth opportunity. There's only one CEO in most companies. Find people who want to grow but who won't be constantly gunning for your job.

Find the right roles for people. A good team is not stagnant, nor should it be. While you need a sturdy foundation on which to build the right group of people in terms of infrastructure, systems, and processes, you should think of employees like the links in a chain. Sometimes you have to take one out and replace it with another, or move the links around to get the right fit and strength. If you have a loyal and enthusiastic person, find what they are good at and put them in a spot where they can shine.

I had an assistant who wasn't working like she was supposed to be. Zoe* was hired to be a chief of staff, a job that required her to spend a lot of time with me, organize my daily engagements and work-related activities, and to manage the team as well. It turned out that she didn't have the specific skill set needed to do the job within our framework. She took a long time to do simple tasks

---

* Name has been changed to protect identity.

and would often have to repeat a job several times before getting it right.

Zoe was also painfully aware that she wasn't doing her job correctly. Not long after an especially stressful day that included an intense photo shoot she came to me and said, "I am going to leave. I feel as if I am disappointing you."

Not so fast. It's time-consuming and costly to replace people, and Zoe seemed to be a good person, loyal and positive. It was not the first time she had said this to me, but instead of accepting her resignation, I offered a possible solution. I had another assistant, Barbara,* who was amazing at being by my side at photo shoots; she loved the hustle of being busy and running around without dropping any balls. I moved Barbara into the position Zoe had, where she thrived.

At the same time, I saw that Zoe might be effective at managing household organizational tasks and house-related projects. These were jobs that could give her autonomy and ownership, but that didn't require the hustle and bustle of working directly with me, inside the pressure cooker.

I suggested to Zoe that she become the house manager, believing that this might put her in a position where she could shine. Unfortunately, it didn't work out. While you do have to try to find the right roles for people, I have found that most of the time things end the way they begin. That's a lesson: Zoe wasn't the right fit anywhere in my organization. We gave it our best shot.

Meanwhile, Barbara has taken over Zoe's old role, and that has worked out well. If you keep people who aren't working out, the chain breaks anyway. Better to remove the link when it is best for everyone to do so.

---

* Name has been changed to protect identity.

Encourage complete honesty and transparency. You never want to have a team that enables members to throw others under the bus to make themselves look good. I have seen this happen, and it bothers me, first because it's wrong, and second, it's not good for morale or productivity. Teams can't be overly protective either, and keep bad news from you. Everyone should feel comfortable saying what's on their mind, bringing up concerns, and having an open discussion about challenges. I want people to be honest with me: tell me what's wrong so we can work on solutions. While I don't have to be told every minute detail of my employees' day, I also never want anyone to be afraid to tell me what's up in the business. I want to train people so that they can work in a way that prevents problems from happening (thinking five steps ahead) or solve problems on their own.

See the big picture. Make sure the people fit together well, complement one another, and complement your skills. For instance, my business manager understands money better than I do, but he doesn't understand the products I make the way I do. We do our best to balance each other's expertise and insight. Thank God my lawyer understands terms of a contract and how to express them in necessary legalese, because I can't. Meanwhile, I do understand legal concepts. I know what questions to ask about a deal. Most of the time our relationship works in a symbiotic fashion. That is how two links that are weak in different ways can strengthen each other.

Make sure everyone is doing their job and sticking to their knitting. When everyone does their job, everyone's job is easier. Of course, we want people to help each other out. We want to build camaraderie and good working relationships. We want people to feel useful and needed. When my driver is less busy in the summer, he can help me out in other ways, moving furniture or doing work outside. But that's not the same as seeing people do someone else's job on a regular basis. I saw that one of my assistants consistently leaned on my housekeeper to help her hang up clothes that we use in the business. That took the housekeeper away from her main job. It was absolutely not fair to her or to me. I spoke to both of them about the issue and we resolved it.

Be constructive with guidance and areas of improvement. Smart, loyal people are worth the consideration of honesty and constructive criticism. They deserve that respect. When I talked about Zoe and Barbara earlier, part of my problem-solving had to do with letting them know not only what they were getting wrong, but being constructive in the ways they could correct it. I was also being specific about what each woman was good at, so we could act from that place in terms of finding the right roles for them in the organization. I talked about how we could put their strengths to work and avoid putting them into positions that taxed their weakest skill sets.

Don't be afraid to cut someone loose. The truth is, the least effective people have the most negative impact on your business. If someone doesn't respond to training, or to a new position, you have to cut them loose. I have had to do this with people who were loyal and kind but I just could not find the right spot for them in the organization. This isn't easy. I wasn't happy—and they weren't either. Consider that it is a relief for the person you are terminating to be released from the stress they obviously feel at being in a job where they may be failing.

B SMART

Your Life Is Like a Chain

The idea that you're only as good as your weakest link is not limited to business. Look at your whole life, and find the weak links. Your grocer, doctor, banker, and dentist, the people who tutor your kids, your plumber, the neighbor's kid who mows your lawn, the high schooler who helps keep your house neat and your laundry folded—any one of them could be the weak link that ends up creating chaos where there should be order. Even in day-to-day life, it's worth thinking of all the people who interact with your team, who are part of the ecosystem that makes your life run smoothly.

The weak link is like the problem child who can pull focus away from the family and bring it down. Even something as seemingly small as a badly trained dog can set in motion a string of mishaps. Here's the inside scoop on my dogs. They've been peeing on carpets and curtains for years. I could not train my precious pup myself, and after a while, that weak link became a bigger issue. Finally, I had to stop and become deliberate about finding the right person to train the dog and train me too—dog trainers are also people trainers. I needed to learn what to do once the trainer was gone and we were on our own! I still find myself going back to the training exercises I learned; it's a work in progress. Sometimes you have to retrain your life or your business in the same way.

Manage to Manage

Avoid the impulse to micromanage. LOL! Easier said than done, especially for entrepreneurs and small-business owners. It is for me, and I don't think I'm alone. I only sweat the small stuff. Getting pulled back into the vines is one of my biggest challenges. Even when you think you're out, you get pulled back in. Not having the right people taking care of the details becomes like the supernatural monster vine in a horror movie. Eventually it wraps itself around your ankle and pulls you under. You need to get to the root of the problem and pull that vine out from where it grows. Too often, I have found myself in the muck, with the vines starting to wind around my legs, because something is either not being done or it's not being done correctly. That's on me: I can identify the problem, but if I fix it by pulling the vine out from the root and replacing it with myself, that doesn't work. You have to identify the problem, pull it out at the root, and find a solution without taking on all the extra work yourself.

I am incredibly fortunate to have a long-standing tight circle of great professionals around me. For more than a decade, they've helped me navigate the sometimes treacherous waters of business and media, and have acted as sounding boards and confidants. Recently I started to build out my administrative team. One thing I've learned through this process, and that most serious business people agree upon, is that finding the right people and managing them is the most difficult part of running a business.

Everybody loves to have the street cred of saying they have an assistant or a staff or employees. I understand that. Hiring is a good sign your business is working and growing, or trying to. Employee growth is one of the boxes on the scorecard of business success. It's enticing. But you do have to remember that it doesn't matter if you have one employee, five employees, or five hundred. Managing them and minimizing weak links down the chain of command is by far the hardest part of running a business. You must be able to delegate wisely, empower people to take ownership of certain areas, accept responsibility, and solve problems autonomously if you want your business *and* your employees to succeed and grow.

Part of my recent effort to bring new people on includes finding an expert social media person to take on the lion's share of responsibility for all my social media posts, from conception to execution. I'm still working on that. I've long struggled with my social media, which includes my own admitted resistance to that world, despite knowing it's a crucial part of the business landscape. Even though there is a lot about social media that I abhor, such as its invasiveness and the way it promotes a false sense of perfection, it's a fact of life if you want to bring your message to an audience. Social media has become a permanent and vital part of the business landscape, and it includes everything: new product development, marketing, corporate communication, brand building, reputation management, customer relations, and more.

"It's everything," Steve Madden told me. "Every month there is something new to explore [in the world of social media]. As someone who didn't grow up with social media, it's not an instinctual thing for me. As a result, I have a team of young people who live and breathe in that world. I'm not on TikTok, but our company is there, and it's fantastic for selling shoes," he says. That's because TikTok and other social media platforms have taken the place of a great deal of advertising, magazines, and even brick-and-mortar retail. Social media is accessible to many people, making the world of social media marketing crowded and competitive. A thirteen-year-old with a smartphone and a sticker machine can make an incredible video that hits a nerve and helps her sell 50,000 stickers in an hour. That's what all of us are up against. Social media has leveled the playing field in many ways, but you *can* have an advantage with a great product and excellent posts, videos, and photography.

When my business became a $100 million enterprise, I realized that I had to become much more deliberate, organized, and professional about my social media effort. It couldn't just be about me frolicking on the beach in a bikini or doing somersaults in my backyard. My posts have to offer something of value, engage my followers, ignite an interest in my

> The weak link is like the problem child who can pull focus away from the family and bring it down.

products, or all of the above. Everything my company puts out has to be excellent from concept to execution. We can't afford to fuck around.

I had one person help with social media who was tactical and strategic about where images should be posted, but whose weakness was in the ability to produce good, properly written captions and create multiple creative solutions for social media. I took the time to assess the kind of link in the chain I needed. Once I determined that I needed someone adept at thinking ahead, seeing the big picture in terms of exploiting creative opportunities, and making posts vibrant, engaging, and informative, I followed up with a search for the best candidates.

Through that process, I met and hired a person who claimed to have the right experience with the social media help I needed: creating, producing, posting, and editing social media images and videos. Great! Since I am not an expert on the technical issues involved in producing social media videos, I had to have faith and trust in the experience she claimed to have.

I had an idea for a fun TikTok video, recreating Eva Perón, the former first lady of Argentina, singing on a balcony, similar to the Broadway show *Evita*. It wasn't something that would move the needle on my business, but if I was going to do it I wanted to do it well. I trusted that my new social media person would do everything necessary to ensure a successful video. TikTok videos are short, less than three minutes, but that doesn't mean they shouldn't look professional. In order to get engagement, videos have to be share-worthy, captivating, and useful. I believed that all I would have to do is show up, put on a dress, and do my thing. The details would be taken care of. It was simply meant to be fun and humorous.

I was dressed and ready. Right before the shoot got underway, I asked my team and the new employee three times (at least, and yes, I am sure I was annoying) how the video would be shot. Normally when creating a TikTok video, you select a song from its playlist and use that music while you film to ensure film and sound are in sync. The social media person told me that the video could be shot and the music added later. Okay, I said, you guys are the millennial experts, you know TikTok, I don't. We did the shoot, and I waited for the results.

Six hours later, when the video was ready to review, my excitement quickly turned to disappointment. It would be obvious to even the most casual viewer that my mouth was not moving in sync with the music, precisely because the music had been recorded outside of the app. It looked like a mistake because it *was* a mistake. That was *exactly* the problem I had envisioned when I asked before we started about how the filming would be done. I get so frustrated when I try to do something, set myself up for success, and it fails.

The video had to be edited, which added more hours to the process for something that was just a minor social media post. At that point I wasn't worrying about the macro part of my $100 million business. There I was, up to my thighs in the weeds, sweating the small stuff. And I still had a weak link! If something that was essentially trivial went so wrong, what would this mean about more major efforts that were not just for fun?

There's a huge extra layer of stress when a big thing goes wrong: it forces you to assume that other things are going wrong. Except you're not sure what, when, or where. It's like seeing a roach on the kitchen counter of a Manhattan apartment. You know it's a sign that there are hundreds more where that one came from, but where are they hiding? And when will they show up? In other words, if the TikTok video got screwed up, what else would go wrong? I needed to fix this problem.

But you know what? This was a great opportunity to show someone new how I like to work and what I want. We sat down together, and I watched the way she edited the film. I talked her through how to edit it, which is hilarious because I know nothing about social media. What happened was that she learned how I work and how I like things to be done. I had to teach her to fish, which is what you have to do anyway. People come to jobs with their own experience, not yours. Keep that in mind, and teach them to fish the way you like to fish. Teach your process.

So many people today describe themselves as social media experts, but experience doesn't always translate into quality. Every organization is different. An individual could have been great at social media for one company, but that doesn't mean they will understand your approach or vision right away, or ever. Training is necessary, no matter the level of experience.

Think about it: a good masseuse can only give one massage at a time. If they teach other people their technique, they can grow their business. Yet they also have to maintain quality control and make sure the techniques are being executed consistently. Even the most seasoned masseuse needs a refresher course to learn new skills and methods. Likewise, any new hire, experienced or otherwise, normally can't hit the ground running at ninety miles an hour or that car is going to crash.

Cracks can become craters without training, but it's easier said than done. Training involves teaching someone your company's language. Don't assume they know it. It's your job to teach them. Every business has a unique approach and its own lingo. Teach in a constructive way, so that the training connects the person to the job and to your company, its culture, and its communication style. Always urge people to be honest about their knowledge. There is a tendency to want to pretend we know everything. I'd rather have a hardworking, loyal, and determined person say to me, "I know how to do this but I have to learn how to do that." That's a person who is teachable.

Stack It

I'm an advocate for what I call stacking, which means squeezing the potential out of every opportunity, which allows for stacked free time as well. For instance, if I am going to be in hair and makeup, which can take a couple of hours, let's shoot five videos or take a hundred photos instead of just one. If I'm going into the city for one appointment, let's make three other appointments to use the day in town efficiently. If Paul and I go out to dinner and we're with the kids, let's make sure we're close to things for the kids to do. It's smart, efficient thinking.

I encourage everyone on my team to think this way, and I advise you to do the same. Stacking strengthens the chain. It can become a game: What can we do to add on to something else? You don't want to get overbooked, so just do what makes sense in the time frame you have. If everyone starts thinking of it as an interesting challenge, you'll get good results. If you take the time to prepare for one thing, you should think of as many ways as you can to exploit that preparation. A brand that includes several product extensions has to use every opportunity to get as many images on film and on to social media as possible. Strike while the iron is hot!

In the case of the TikTok video, I already had my hair and makeup done, or what I call my "glam." Outside of necessity for work I never get glam done; I *despise* it. I would rather feel healthy and clean with my hair pulled back and no makeup than made up to the nines. Since I was going to be dressed up, what else could we do while I was in Super Bethenny mode beyond just the TikTok? We could get so many social media posts done—enough for a week or more of posts. We could stage additional photographs with my products. A lunch shoot could highlight my salad dressing. When I change back into my sweatpants, a cozy, relaxed shot with my coffee and one or more of my candles glowing in the background could be a great social media post with a weekend vibe. I could show off my jeans and sunglasses in other photos. There were many possibilities, but I was the only one who seemed to be thinking about these possibilities. I had to train my team to think like I do, meaning to try to maximize every opportunity and be efficient.

Teach your team to be proactive rather than reactive. I want to encourage my team to always be proactive. I want them to be *better* than me at thinking about photo shoots or social media opportunities, at least ten blocks ahead of me.

An instructive situation occurred during a baking shoot we had planned for the Home Shopping Network. My team was clear about and well aware of everything that would be needed to create a successful segment. As I mentioned earlier, clarity about roles and responsibilities is key in creating a strong chain. In this particular case, the immersion blender should have been on the counter, the necessary ingredients all portioned out and lined up, mixing bowls clean and ready to use, and the product I was selling front and center. Nothing was set up when I arrived on set, which in this case was my home kitchen. That fact alone, that we were not filming in an unfamiliar studio, meant it should have been easy for people already working in my house to grab everything necessary from my cabinets. Everything is on hand, and I have an extremely well-organized kitchen.

Eventually one of my team members pulled together the needed equipment, but as I started to create the recipe—*on camera*—I realized that other items I needed to make the cookies were not within reach. This threw me off my game, to say the least. If the support isn't there, it doesn't matter how good a cook I am, or how spontaneous and fun I am on camera. The weakest link was now calling the shots, and that's not good. We had to scramble to get through that particular live shoot. And yes, I was back in the weeds, flustered and frustrated.

This was another chance for me to talk to the team about how to think about a project and prepare for it. Train and train again.

Some people may say that I did it backwards; that I should have found the right people first, before my product lines exploded, and trained all of them. In theory, that's a great idea. I agree. Except that reality isn't as accommodating as conjecture. Expansion can happen in quick spurts, often after months or even years of a slow build. Your needs change and evolve. You don't always know when a business will take off, usually after years of building and laying groundwork. There is also some work that has unpredictable elements, and you need people who can anticipate on their own and solve problems on the fly. And sometimes you have to train while doing—another example of flying the rocket while you're building it.

Yes, you have to be prepared for potential outcomes by building a decent foundation at the beginning stages of a business; otherwise, the house will crumble. However, you can't always do things in the perfect order. As much as we'd like it to, real life doesn't work that way. There are always wild cards and unpredictable events. As you grow, expand, and evolve, some links will weaken and others will strengthen. No business (or life) reaches a point where all the links are consistently strong and sturdy. There's always a duck wandering away from the row. Vigilance is required to spot weaknesses and address them without putting yourself in micromanagement mode. And yes, that's on me and the senior leaders on my team.

> Teach people to fish and they will thrive.

I have gotten better at communicating clearly what I want and expect, and as a result, I have a stronger team, and we're doing a good job of teaching new people to fish Bethenny-style.

Penny Wise, Pound Foolish

One temptation that can also lead to broken links is trying to save money in the wrong ways: penny wise and pound foolish. You often end up throwing good money after bad if you don't make quality investments in systems, staff, operations, and materials. Hiring the wrong person because they cost less than another person can and often does end up costing you more time and money, in the form of mistakes made and time wasted. I also don't mind spending money for value, while I detest wasting money on anything, from clothes to dog groomers to employees. I'd rather have one somewhat expensive employee who takes genuine ownership of the job than two less costly average people.

Another example of penny wise, pound foolish happens quite often during home renovations. For instance, using subpar materials because they seem affordable can cost you so much money in the long run, because cheaper materials can fail more quickly than high-quality materials. That does not mean that savings and quality are mutually exclusive. My apartment in the city was done properly and in a cost-effective way. I renovated the apartment the way I wanted to, but that didn't mean all the materials and labor I put into it were costly. I found the best materials I could afford within my budget. I spent money where it was important (craftsmanship, fixtures) and saved where I could preserve and restore what was good in the apartment (woodwork, flooring). I can go into any house or apartment and assess what is good and can stay and what needs to be replaced. I can see potential in diamonds in the rough. I try to understand those things before hammer hits nail and the project begins.

When I renovated my house in the Hamptons, I approached it in the wrong way, which I regret. It was my first time fixing a house; I had no experience and designed as I went. I felt rushed. There were so many things I should have done from the beginning, such as refinishing the floors throughout the house so they were consistent. Granted, I didn't know as much about renovation as I know now, but I did make mistakes that I thought were cost savers. In the long run, it took more money to fix the weak links than it would have to do it right from the start.

Whether it's businesses or real estate or relationships, sometimes you have to stop and think about how much you're going to invest in something. Are the weak links fixable or replaceable? If they aren't, you have to do some serious introspection. Consider how far you're willing to go, because you can get upside down quickly. It's humbling.

The weak link could show itself in times of crisis as well. It could be that you're getting sued for something, or you receive an unexpected bill or expense, just enough to bring the whole system down while you figure it out, because the weak link is not having a good lawyer or not having a reserve fund to cover unexpected expenses—but you just don't realize it until the shit hits the fan.

Ultimately, you have to be honest with yourself about what you want your business to be and how you can realistically achieve it. Mike Tyson said that everyone has a plan until they get punched in the mouth. This insight is applicable to business. Examine all your systems before a crisis hits: Do you have the right people? Are your reserves robust enough to see you through lean times or take care of an unexpected emergency? If not, now is the time to make sure you're secure, not when you're scrambling and distracted. It's similar to being five steps ahead and planning for the unexpected.

Finally, I want to close with an important insight that Steve Madden offered when I interviewed him. "I always believed that if I made great shoes that people wanted to buy, everything would take care of itself. I wouldn't have to worry about lawyers, profit and loss statements, and accountants. All I had to do was make shoes that girls wanted to wear. That is still the overriding philosophy of my company today. When we get distracted by business deals, we go back to the original idea of making great shoes that people want to buy."

In fact, you do have to worry about the other things, which is why you need strong links in your chain—so you can do what *you're* good at doing: working on your business, creating value with fresh ideas, and delighting your audience or customers. That's how Steve Madden became a mogul—by finding the right people to keep his chain strong. That's what I want to create—a place for my ideas to grow, my relief work and philanthropic efforts to rise, and my family to bloom.

It's all possible for us if we stick to our mission and our driving motivators. Remember that success is not just about the money. Money is just part of the scorecard for how well you're doing. When you're mindful about what you need and want, the weak links can be repaired or replaced. They will be easier to find and faster to fix.

8

Keep Your Circle Tight

WHEN IT COMES TO INTERPERSONAL RELATIONSHIPS, BUSINESS or otherwise, there are three kinds of people: extroverts, who appear to have loads of friends and associates, although none of them seem especially close; introverts, who have a few select close friends and colleagues, and tend to keep to themselves; and a middle ground, the people who are outer directed and friendly, but can also entertain themselves and have best friends. I'm the last type of person. Another expression for this third type is Shop Closed; or Police Tape, Do Not Cross. I'm not making too many new friends at this point in my life. And this can be unsettling for some people, because I'm dispassionate about it.

There are people who say, *Oh dear, Bethenny doesn't have many friends.* I *do* have friends—serious, long-lasting friends that I consider family—and I don't keep a scorecard. Quality versus quantity is key for me. This idea came up frequently on the *Housewives.* I would observe some of the people on the show who had dozens and dozens of fake friends. I knew this because I'd run into some of those so-called friends, and they would trash the other person. If they are talking about someone to me, then they are talking about me to someone else. That is not a real friend. There has never been one time in my life that one of my best friends has ever said a bad thing about me to somebody else. I intend on keeping it that way by keeping my circle tight.

It's not surprising that my default button is insular and private. Even though I'm tough as nails, I'm also vulnerable. I was an only child, and I often found myself alone and left to my own devices because my mother and stepdad were not always around or attentive. Home life was often ephemeral, nontraditional, and dysfunctional, with gambling and the world of horse racing thrown in. I've seen every kind of abuse—from physical to alcohol to drugs to eating disorders. As a consequence, I grew up quickly, developed a thick skin, and was a mature child. I did adult things as a young person. It started with me going to a club called the Rafters in Saratoga.

When I was thirteen, my mother gave me a fake ID from a nanny or au pair that I would use to get into the club. I'd also use the ID to frequent clubs like Area and the Palladium in Manhattan. I dressed in a way that was sophisticated for my age, but not provocative or revealing, and I behaved with a maturity far beyond my years. As a result, I never had a problem getting into any club. I would take the train safely in and out of the city at that age. I've never said this before, but I tried drugs in a private room at the Palladium when I was fourteen years old. Thankfully, I don't have an "addictive personality," otherwise I would have been the perfect profile for substance abuse. I don't like to feel out of control, and that's how drugs make one feel. The dirtiness, desperation, and dishonesty that surround drugs have always turned me off. Make sure you teach your children to see drugs through that filter, because peer pressure is great around drugs and young people. Some people are also predisposed to addiction and have a different battle.

We also moved frequently. I have lost count, but I believe I attended thirteen different schools before starting college. That meant I was always the new kid in class, which I found to be a welcome challenge, a fresh start. I'm not especially awkward socially, which some of my friends find ironic because I'm open about the fact that I consider myself insular and a loner. I often go so far as to describe myself as antisocial, in the sense that I'd rather be home with my little family or by myself, in my PJs, working on my businesses, cooking with my daughter, practicing yoga, or taking solo walks on the beach, rather than schmoozing at a cocktail party or attending red carpet events. Of course, I did the red carpet as a means to an end back in the day, but that was work for me. Business, writing, and my podcast are my creative and emotional outlets.

Quality versus quantity is key.

Know Who You Are and Know Who Your Friends Are

Being well known, whether it's on a large national or international stage or a small one, like your town or company, can give a false sense of who your friends are. There are fake people everywhere, and some of them can be seductive. I don't mean romantically (although that can happen too). I'm referring to people who can fool you into thinking they care about you when they don't. There will always be some degree of bad energy around you: people who are jealous or spiteful. You can't let yourself be surrounded by toxic energy, because it's unhealthy and it's also contagious.

You may enter into a circle and think, *Oh, wow, I'm around people who are just like me. I found my tribe!* You make friends quickly—this can happen in the workplace, in a neighborhood, a mommy and me group, a reality TV show, or anywhere. But then it's a matter of time before you start to hear people in the group gossip about other people in the group, or people start stabbing one another in the back. Egos clash, jealousies arise, competition begins. The ugliness starts to emerge. That's when you need your tight circle to go back to your cocoon. That's a crucial lesson I learned.

When I talked to the youngest (to date) mogul I have featured on my podcast, social media (30-plus million followers across numerous social media platforms) and internet personality, entrepreneur, and investor Josh Richards, we shared the value of this lesson, which is usually learned the hard way. He was nineteen when I talked to him, but he had a profound and mature view of fame. "Fame is a gift and curse. There is not one kid in their senior year of high school who would say, oh, I don't want to drop out of high school, move into a mansion in LA, and post social media content. But for the three and a half years I was building my social media platform, I was being made fun of in school. Lunchtime would be the worst part of the day. I had my friend group, and before I started doing social media I was a pretty popular kid because I played sports. That's how you become popular in a small town. When I did actually drop out of high school and move to LA, I thought, wow, now I'm around people like me. Friends were made quickly. But I also saw fake people stabbing each other in the back. I learned to keep friends tight. Stick with your inner circle. Everyone in my house is someone I would take a bullet for. I don't need to hang with anyone else."

It's amazing that someone so young has learned this important lesson so early in his career and life.

Josh is right too. There are so many watered-down, filtered versions of people running around the entertainment industry, it's the absolute majority. I am 100 percent the exception to this, no question. It bothers me when someone doesn't come across as real or authentic. I am 100 percent unafraid to say what I think, be who I am, and have difficult conversations. It is what it is, but I also know what fake looks like, and fake people are not going to be part of my innermost circle. I'm careful to create a circle that's not just tight, but made up of people, whether personal friends or trusted business associates, who are authentic, sincere, and have positive energy. I don't let anyone into my bubble who dulls my sparkle because of their own insecurities, fears, and anxieties, and neither should you.

If toxic people somehow enter your realm, whether because of a business deal or a work arrangement in which you are not in control of who all the players are, you need your tight circle, your cocoon, for a reality check.

When I interviewed Hillary Clinton for my podcast, she said something that resonates so strongly in terms of having a tight and trusted circle, about accepting supporters and critics without creating a false sense of yourself. It was advice from woman to woman, but it was also wise and motherly, nurturing that we can all benefit from.

"You have people who just adore you and follow you, and model themselves after you," she said, "and then you've got people who will complain and critique you." I think we can all relate to that. "You can't get pushed to the extreme, you can't believe all the adulation and the best about yourself, and you certainly should not buy into all the negativity and the hate and all the rest that goes with the critics. You have to chart your own course. At the end of the day, that's all you can do. Just be who you are, for better, for worse, good times and bad, and the people who get you will get you and they'll know that you are an imperfect human being. Do the best you can to get through the day, to be fair and good to people around you. At the end of it, you've got to be happy and satisfied with yourself," she continued. Wow! *Yes.* Comedian Ellen DeGeneres told me the same thing: Don't believe all the love, all the hype. Your circle should be made up of people who understand you, and you them. Everyone else is window dressing.

It can take time to curate the right group. Enter friendships slowly. Take small bites. Friends should also never be used as currency. My friends don't care if I'm well-known, they don't watch half my shows, and couldn't care less about my media presence. Our friendship is based on who we are as people, and I can trust them. You have to have a strong filter. I can probably count on two hands the people I trust, and the close friends I have in my life. I'm content with this. I'd rather have a tight circle in my personal and business life than have a million friends who mean nothing to me. The three most important elements of any relationship, whether it's a BFF, a romantic someone, spouse, or business partner are honesty, loyalty, and respect. These can't be found in more than a handful of people at any one time.

Paul is similar to me in this way. We love who we love, and we love hard. We don't care what other people think of this, and it's liberating to not have that kind of sensitivity to what other people think of my personal life. What other people think of me is none of my business. Do what you want to do, be who you want to be, without caring what others think. It's a liberating feeling, and it's not selfish. If it feels disingenuous to do something, then don't do it. I don't get gifts for people because they've given me a gift. I give gifts because I want to.

At every party I have, I count on the same ten or twenty people to come and enjoy. They know each other and trust one another.

We can all be ourselves, and that makes entertaining down to earth and relaxing. I take pride in the fact that all of my friends love my other friends and have become friends with each other. People call this friend-jumping, and I love and encourage it. Why wouldn't I want my friends to know each other? I'd rather they talk to each other and see each other socially; I don't need to be the hub for everything. Let them all be good friends with one another, and I can see them at Skinnygirl events or TV show parties. It's just a nice, good group of ten to twenty people.

Because I'm an insular, introverted person, I try to never be out of my comfiest clothes unless I have to be. Television changed that for me somewhat, which was good for me because it forced me to put on makeup and get out of the house looking decent. Before I was on TV, I would always be in my PJs. I remember going to Starbucks with pimple medicine on my face, wearing my cow print pajamas. I was still a homebody, even when I was living in a studio apartment. It was hard to get me out at night. I'd tell myself that I should go out to dinner or make plans with a friend, but the effort usually entailed hours of anxiety.

That's why, even though I have reached a level of public recognition, it still shocks me that famous people know who I am. I remember attending a night-before-the-Oscars party where there were many famous people around. I couldn't believe it when A-list people attending were aware of me, said hello, and called me by name. At another Mark Burnett–hosted event, Lady Gaga said, "Hello, Bethenny!" Huh? I thought to myself, *Why and how does Lady Gaga know who I am?*

When Donald Trump was running for president the first time, he stopped me while I was doing the walk of shame through the lobby of a building after spending the night upstairs at a friend's apartment. It was 7:45 in the morning. I was holding my two dogs on leashes. I was wearing a cut-off sweatshirt under a jacket, over-the-knee spike-heeled boots, and my jewelry was in a glass. Mascara was running down my face. And there's Donald Trump, saying, "Bethenny," to me and telling his aides, "Take care of her. She's the most important person in this building." What?! I was horrified.

So weird and shocking.

I have to say that I feel awkward most of the time when I am recognized by anyone, which I know sounds crazy because I am easily identified even when I'm not wearing makeup (which is the majority of the time when I am living my life). I do have many fans who know what I look like, and I so appreciate them. Most of the press probably know me on sight. For someone who feels like an introvert most of the time, it's jarring to be noticed. I still don't go out that much. In terms of public awareness, I think people can become a bit different when it happens, no matter the scale of the recognition. There are different reactions to it: some people embrace it, and other people tend to become more reclusive because of it, and I think I am a bit more of the latter.

Being well known makes me a little less comfortable in public because you never know when someone is staring, or looking at you, or taking pictures of you. That doesn't seem natural to me, which is interesting. There are people who desire that kind of attention, but I don't. I like my fans and respect them and the connection we have. But at the same time, it's intrusive when paparazzi take your picture when you're just walking down the street with your child to get ice cream. My fifteen minutes are definitely fading because I don't do as much television, and I don't want to be written about unless I am promoting something.

Those who embrace their fame put a lot of time into it. I'm not one of them, but I have seen famous people on vacation, posing for photographers with or in front of their partner. They always seem to be camera ready, no matter what they're doing. This would be so embarrassing and phony for me. If I was with my fiancé, Paul, and I did this, I don't know how he would tolerate it, or if he would. I hope he wouldn't. I have to admit my practical side comes through here too—if you are into being photographed when you're out in public, you also have to embrace the fact that it takes two hours to get ready just on the off chance that there may be a random photograph snapped of you as you emerge from Starbucks. I don't do hair and makeup now unless I'm getting paid for it. I'm glad that I've never trapped myself in that vicious cycle. I'm happy with who I am and am honest about it. Most of the time, when I *am* out and about, it is what it is. Sometimes I look scary and sometimes I don't. But it's always my decision, and I don't care what people think about me when I'm living my life.

> Surround yourself with people of integrity, good intentions, and excellent reputations, who will inspire you and reflect on to you.

Make the Connection

The combination of my safe space being a small circle and my own dislike of the party circuit made networking a challenge when I was building my business. It's still not easy for me to work a room with the high energy that requires, but I've gotten better at it. My publicist helps me decide if I have to go to an event or not, and I will go if it's something my daughter will love, or if it is good for my business. But I'd much rather stay home. When I was building my wheat-, egg-, and dairy-free baking business, BethennyBakes,

I'd force myself to attend events and social functions in Manhattan and the Hamptons. As long as I kept focused on why I was there—to raise awareness of my brand—and didn't get dragged into meaningless small talk, I was okay. I'm not the kind of person who wants to waste time on pointless conversations anyway. But still, staying focused was exhausting: smiling, introducing myself to strangers, being up and energetic and on my feet at public or society events was and is hard work. It's necessary to have a wide network of people from a variety of disciplines and with a diverse range of knowledge for business whether you are starting out or established, even if your close friends remain a small group.

It's nice to know that I'm undeniably respected in the industry by executives and other industry people. When it comes to business and social events, I'm goal-oriented. When I was going out to meet people to date, I was goal-oriented and interested in meeting someone with whom I would share my phone number. When I am at a business event, I focus on making connections. Over time I believe I have built a reputation as someone who doesn't want to know you because I want something from you. But I *do* want to connect and make things happen.

I have always connected, built the mosaic, and laid the bricks to make a path. As an example, when I was running BethennyBakes and eager to get on the Food Network as a natural food chef, I went to the Sundance Film Festival in Park City, Utah, and hustled to make connections. This was when I was still a nobody. I was in the gifting suites, connecting, handing out my cookies, and meeting people. There were some local people who owned a restaurant that held a little-known event called Chef Dance. It was low-key in the beginning. Each night, a locally known chef would cook a free, multi-course dinner for guests. I pushed and pushed them to allow me to take over the event and host it. Finally, I convinced them to let me host the following year's dinner. I was an expert party planner and was able to get them so much press. I helped the restaurant secure well-known chefs from all over the country. I kept in touch with those chefs all year because I wanted to be on the Food Network and I wanted to be a successful chef.

So even though I don't want to have a crazy social life and a million insincere friends, I've always been a connector—the two things are not mutually exclusive. I met Kevin Mazur, my ex-boyfriend and a well-known and respected celebrity photographer, at Sundance. He was the one who walked me down my first red carpet and persuaded other photographers to take pictures of me even though I was unknown. Whenever friends I knew from childhood or from my hustle who worked in PR had a party, I accepted those invitations and connected. I tried to be relevant because I wanted to be something someday. I have never forgotten the people who were nice to me then, because they didn't have to be. Those who were kind and gracious have a place in my heart.

Bottom line is that I was always connecting. I didn't think the people I was connecting with were my friends or would become my friends—although some of them have become good friends. Icing on the wheat-, dairy-, and egg-free cake! For me, it was about making things happen and finding ways to do the kind of work I wanted to do. Connecting is how I ended up on *The Apprentice*, the *Housewives*, my talk show, and my podcast. It's how everything has always happened. I continue today, but now it's on a different level.

I use connecting in my relief work. When people were just starting to talk about the shortages of masks and other protective equipment and material during the early days of the COVID shutdown in 2020, I started to investigate how I could help. If I could find masks, we would donate them. The best way to do this is to connect to people where their hearts are. It has to be meaningful; otherwise it feels inauthentic. Create connectivity to people with transparency. Focus on the things that are important to them: if you're delivering food in a crisis, you say to one person, do you want to deliver food to the local Chabad because you're Jewish, or do you want to distribute masks through the churches because you're Christian, or do you want to help the children's hospital because you are involved in early childhood development, and so on.

With COVID relief, I put people together this way. Matthew McConaughey helped Texas because that's where his roots are. Billy Joel wanted to help Long Island, so I put him in touch with people who could facilitate that. I communicated with all my contacts because I had credibility as a businesswoman, and I could not let that go to waste if my clout could be used to help people who were desperate for life-saving equipment.

So *yes*, you do have to network in life and work, but don't get caught up in the social aspect of connections or be fooled by it, because it can pull you off track, create an illusion of friendships where none exist, and prevent you from meeting your goals.

B SMART

You Are Who You Surround Yourself With

The people in your life are reflective of who you are, so I am careful who I associate with personally and professionally. Paul helped me get out of a possible partnership in one of my potential wine deals, because he discovered that an unsavory character was involved. An association with this person could have been bad for me, but we realized early on that it was not a good situation.

I've met so many men who have been publicly revealed to be predators, some recently, and for multiple offenses. Most of the people who are found out to be questionable, aka scumbags, always seemed like that to me. It was obvious, in fact. None of these so-called "revelations" about the bad behavior of powerful people surprised me in the least. When an actor feigns surprise that she has worked with people who were doing terrible things and had no idea, she is lying. How could I know someone was not right after one meeting and someone else can work with the same person for decades and claim to have never suspected a thing? Come on! The sleazebag in all of them was clear to me after one casual meeting.

The problem is that we can all get so thirsty to be near fame and to be near the light. It's human nature, I get it. But you also have to be conscious of who you are associating with, because whatever they are radiating, good or bad, is rubbing off on you. Surround yourself with people of integrity, good intentions, and excellent reputations, who will inspire you and reflect well on you. If you surround yourself with predators, those who are dishonest, that's going to stain you. I think most of us know in our guts who is right and who is wrong. Follow your gut. Don't do things that your instinct tells you feel wrong, because somehow, some way they will come back to haunt you. As *Housewives* alum Caroline Manzo would always say, "If you hang around with garbage you start to stink!" Words to live by.

Karma will show up in life and business. You might get away with cheating, shortcuts, not being straightforward and above board, but karma will show up. It might take years, but it does show up.

Keep It Real

To be clear, I'm not telling you to ditch all your casual friends or to stop being nice to the people at work, or anything of the sort. Of course you can and should be authentically friendly and kind. That's called being a good human being. There's a great deal of interest, even obsession, on the internet about who I'm friends with from the *Housewives* and who I'm not, who I follow and who I don't. It's ridiculous, because while I have definitely had emotional moments with my TV relationships, my real friends are timeless and my work colleagues are unique. I am going to shoot straight. There will always be a limit to relationships made in certain circumstances. You may have good friends at work, and they are real, but those friendships can and do fall away once you leave that job. Made-for-television relationships are real in the moment but not always lasting. It is the nature of the game. Teresa and Danielle's friendship on the *Housewives* will always be off and on. The Dina and Caroline relationship on the *Housewives* will always be on and off. Jill Zarin and I have had a similar rocky road. These are relationships that are created for the show.

I always want to be able to talk honestly and be myself around people. I can't stand tiptoeing around. I'm up front with everybody, whether they're my close friend or in my tight business circle or not, and I let the chips fall where they may. But at the end of the day your friends are the ones who take you at face value. The value of good friends can't be overstated.

The people that you can count on every day and who count on you—those people are fewer than you think. So, what I *am* telling you is think about who makes you feel empowered and special; who is there for you when you need it. The best relationships enable both parties to do great things. For instance, who has your back at work? Who gives you the best advice? Who listens?

When my daughter Bryn is having drama with her friends and there's some jealousy or competition coming up, I always say be nice and be discreet. Don't call anybody out. Don't say, we're not friends anymore, because you will be friends again. It's tempting to let people know that you're aware of what they did or said, or that you see them behaving badly. It's not worth it. It's usually better to keep your mouth shut. And don't be all about the boys, because girls can cause so much strife and anger when it comes to boys and who likes whom.

Instead, I tell my daughter to play the game; keep it clean and keep it nice. Always know whom you're dealing with; put your radar up and know who people are from a distance. You don't have to let them know you know who they are. Just understand who is the most competitive, who's a copycat, and which one tends to be jealous. This one is a good friend, and this one is boring but she's a good person. This one is a lot of fun, and this one gets in trouble all the time. Find a couple of friends whom you will maintain for your whole life. With everyone else, keep your cards close to your vest. This is good advice for grown-ups too.

Now, don't think I'm saying that friendships or work relationships are one-sided and only about what's in them for you. You have to feel as if you're giving something to the relationship that's meaningful to the other person. Otherwise they're not going to stick around if they aren't getting something back that makes them feel good, and valued, and honored. Sometimes you have to play the game. Many relationships feel real in the moment, and you want to believe they will last. I have been friends with all the Housewives in the moment, but when competition arises, it's not a good recipe for friendship.

You also have to understand where people are coming from. Kelly Ripa said it straight regarding a girl in my child's classroom.

155

She told me that you have to think about where that child came from and what her experiences have been when judging behavior. Exhibit understanding and compassion. Everyone doesn't come from the same place.

You also have to understand yourself and what matters to you. I have learned that I'm a lot to handle. Hard to believe, right? Only kidding. During a recent interview, I mentioned to journalist Tamron Hall that relationships are about finding people who can handle you. That took her aback. It's the truth. I am a strong woman, and not everyone can keep up with that, or feels comfortable with it, including other women. But it's the truth, my truth. I need people around me who know how to deal with me. I'm intense. I need my friends, colleagues, and my partner to understand the level of my career and the energy it takes, because it's not easy to be in a relationship with someone who is so driven and so passionate. My business is all-encompassing, and I need people who can pull me out of that sometimes. We all need people like that in our lives, and there are never going to be droves of people who can be that understanding and plugged into your personality. It's a lot to expect from most people, and only a few will make the cut.

> Develop your filter and become expert at identifying who has your back and who doesn't.

Don't Connect the Dots

Another mistake people make in connecting is connecting too many dots for too many people. Yes, I know it sounds completely counterintuitive and contradictory, but it's not. Let me explain.

There are people who believe it's okay to share what they are doing, and who they know, with people outside of their tight and trusted circle. It is tempting to do that. It's *not* okay. People will say things like, oh yeah, I know Jane and she knows you, and she's doing this and I'm doing that. Why do you have to share that information with people who will use it to their own advantage? What you have to realize is that everyone has their own agenda, and it's not always aligned with yours. When you give too much away, it can compromise your plans. People use connected dots as currency. For instance, if you share a new idea with someone outside of your trusted circle, and also provide the names of the people who are working with you on it, the person you're talking to can use that information to create or forward a competing or similar idea. It's unnecessary to share information with people who are not involved in your business. Yes, you can network, but you can do it without spilling your beans.

You may feel you're just being honest and sharing information with someone, but they may be thinking to themselves, *she's doing what* or *she knows him*? If you know this and it's a friend of yours, fine, but be careful about what you say and to whom. Anytime someone volunteers to connect dots for me, it allows me to figure out certain things about them and how certain business deals or mistakes were made. For instance, someone I meet could share an experience they had in the jeans business that would help me in my jeans business. They could mention people whom I don't know personally but whom I may want to connect with. That could be valuable information, because it allows me to connect the dots in my mind. I advise against doing this, because revealing too much information about your plans that may or may not come to fruition makes you vulnerable.

The only time I ever got in trouble on the *Housewives* was when I connected the dots for someone in a moment of weakness by giving them information they ended up using against me. Why give people ammunition? Why give them a chance to point out that you failed or didn't come through on an idea you're thinking of? It can cause a lot of animosity among casual friends and colleagues. You have to be careful.

Because so few people follow this rule, it means you can sit back and listen to people connect dots for you. That is how you garner useful information. The iconic Wall Street rascal Gordon Gekko from the movie *Wall Street* said if you're not on the inside, you're on the outside. In business I absolutely feel that you have to know what's going on, but you don't have to be the one spreading the news.

It's interesting, but I find that women in particular can't help but share information, especially if they drink or are in a casual social setting. They can sing like canaries. I will absolutely tell you what I ate for lunch, but I am not going to tell you whom I met, what they said, and what I might be working on with them. I've been candid in this book, but only about those things that I feel are important in getting my point across, or that help you understand the way my tools work.

On the *Housewives*, the castmates, and even the public and the press, wanted to know my salary. No one would even dare to ask because they knew I would never, ever tell them. I am a vault. Even if you tell just one person, they will rat you out—but at least you know who is on your side and who isn't. The fewer dots you connect with the fewest number of people, the tighter your circle, and the safer you are. With my closest friends, I connect every dot because they are completely trustworthy.

I put a great deal of energy and thought into the important relationships in my life and business. I cherish family and close friends. I respect my business partners. I'm an excellent mother and put a lot of love into the relationship with my daughter. That effort is in large part why the close relationships I enjoy are so amazing and satisfying. Everybody else? I wish them well; I wish them happiness and health. But at the end of the day, it's my circle that matters.

As I wrote this I was thinking about my upcoming wedding. Weddings are always fraught with all sorts of emotions. I have come to the realization that this time, there will not be a cast of hundreds at the event. There will be people whom I know will be shocked that they were not invited, and those who will totally understand why they were left off the guest list. I'm ready for the disappointment of some. This wedding is not about staging an event. It's a precious moment, and Paul and I want it to be filled with positive energy and love. I will not tolerate inviting people out of a sense of obligation to do so. I understand that this is often the purpose of a wedding party—to check the boxes on every family member and distant cousin, high school buddy, or professional colleague. I also don't need someone standing in the back of a room criticizing the chicken dish or the floral arrangements or my dress. My best friends would never do that, and they know who they are.

As we go through business and life we meet all sorts of people, good, bad, and indifferent. As always, go with your gut instinct; it rarely lets you down. Get in tune with your instincts by developing your filter and becoming expert at identifying who has your back and who doesn't. Answer these questions honestly, because you *do* know the answers: Who is loyal and who isn't? Who tells you the truth every time, and who can be counted on to bullshit you? Who is there when you need help, and who only wants to connect when things are good? That's the shoulder to cry on versus the cold shoulder! Who listens without interrupting and offers honest advice when requested? The answers tell you all you need to know about your circle.

9

Run the Marathon

BUSINESS AND LIFE, LIKE MOTHERHOOD, ARE MARATHONS, NOT sprints. We're in it for the long haul. How you manage the inevitable obstacles, pitfalls, problems, and crises and the burnout and stress makes all the difference in how well you and your business will survive. Nothing is easy all the time, and you have to be prepared to go the distance if you want to succeed. Your response to challenging circumstances and unpredictable events defines you. Trip-ups and face-plants along the way should only sideline you temporarily while you heal and come back stronger. Maneuvering through the marathon of life, and facing the inevitable obstacles and problems on the path which are often out of your control, takes fortitude and a strong belief in what's right for you.

I've learned a great deal about crisis management from working through difficult circumstances in my own life and business, and I have honed my understanding of how to deal with crisis through my philanthropic efforts focused on helping people after natural disasters. It's clear to me that surviving a struggle, solving problems, and coming out the other side are invaluable for both personal and professional growth. The worst of times can be a test of your ability to apply the tools you've learned during the good times. You *can* create positives out of negative experiences. And you will get stronger.

I talked to Niren Chaudhary about this. A longtime food industry executive who became CEO of Panera Bread Company in 2019, he was just getting his head around the large company—there are nearly 2,300 Panera restaurants in the United States—when the pandemic hit the hospitality industry hard in early 2020. He watched as half of his business evaporated in the week the country shut down in an effort to flatten the virus's curve. At that time, no one imagined two weeks would turn into more than a year of closings and business losses.

Did Niren call it quits? No.

"Our mindset was, how can we use this unprecedented event as a catalyst to become better and stronger, and establish greater trust with our stakeholders?" He says there were many moments of learning and reflection, and he had a few important insights that not only helped save and improve the business, but that can help you think about difficult moments in your professional and personal trajectory too. "The first is to remain calm. There's a tendency to want to jump into action mode and do something. Instead, take the opportunity and step back, especially when there is no playbook," he said. "Identify what is truly important for the Panera team. For us it was first the safety of customers and employees, and second, the protection and preservation of the brand and business."

Panera made some hard decisions, like temporarily reducing its workforce by 35,000, and permanently shuttering a handful of stores. In doing so, he thought about the filters the company would use to make these tough calls. "One was that even if you do hard things, you can do them with compassion and respect. We think of Panera as a family, and families sacrifice for each other. What sacrifices would be made in order to keep people employed and safe, and how could we ensure the survival of the business? Third, let's not burn the furniture. This too shall pass. Let's not overreact. Finally, how can we use the experience to become stronger, accelerate the changes we were thinking would take three years to three months?"

Just one year after the pandemic started, Panera was profitable again.

Some of the best advice Niren offers applies to anyone's giant obstacle or difficult situation, even if you're not running a billion-dollar food company. "Sit still," Niren says. "Collect yourself. Pick a lane. Focus on what you can do and not on the noise around you." Worry less about how long a problem will last; focus on what you can do in the moment that is productive and helpful. He uses the metaphor of windmills versus bunkers. Harness the wind from the storm and use it instead of hiding from it in a shelter. I love that analogy, and I try to live my life that way—by using the storm, not hiding from it.

Designer Rebecca Minkoff harnessed that wind when her business took a devastating hit during the pandemic and the civil unrest that followed in many cities. Every single one of the stores they sold to canceled orders, and her business dropped by 50 percent almost overnight. Layoffs and furloughs were inevitable, and two of her own stores had to shut permanently. Her Los Angeles store was devastated by riots. She didn't give up. In fact, she started over, focusing on her website, which has helped her pull in new business, including lucrative wholesale partners. More than 80 percent of her workforce is back.

Think like Niren and Rebecca, and so many other business powerhouses who have tackled stormy times. Don't let obstacles sideline your business or life—problems are an inevitable part of the journey to sustained success. Confront problems calmly. Grace under pressure helps you make better decisions and gives you the fortitude and courage it takes to right a wrong and ask for what is rightfully yours.

I've overcome some pretty crazy things in my life; I could fill another book with stories about all the dragons I've had to slay. What follows are just a few examples that show how a strong moral compass, a sense of right and wrong, and tenacity pay off when dealing with the rocks on the road.

> **Never accept anything less than what you deserve.**

Nip Problems in the Bud

One of the ways you earn a strong and respected reputation is by not allowing people to take advantage of you in the first place. It might be easier in the moment to let a wrong slide, but in the long run it's not good for you professionally, personally, or emotionally. Knowing someone got away with a transgression can and will suck the life out of you. And people who get away with murder once will do it again. Be part of the solution by stopping problems in their tracks, before they worsen. And by the way, most people are not confrontational; they are ultimately scaredy-cats, so know that when you call someone on a legit concern, most will back down.

I had to do this recently, after one of my partners communicated in an unprofessional way to the people I work with, and said things about me that were inaccurate. When the partnership process didn't seem to be working in the way that they imagined, an email was sent to some members of my staff complaining about it, perhaps thinking that the partner could pound its chest to my staff, as a power play to get more leverage over me to change the process.

When my team showed me the email, I was shocked, first, because the person wasn't candid enough to send those concerns directly to me, and second, because so much of what was in the email was erroneous. This partnership was lucrative for me; I was being paid a great deal of money to partner with this company. I have worked with other partners in the same category before who have been respectful, and they worked well. This partner felt they were not getting exactly what they wanted out of our collaboration. On the other hand, the key players in the company weren't attending meetings; they were sending less experienced people to handle discussions with me. In fact, the letter came from someone who hadn't participated in any dialogue, despite being one of the partner company's top people. The tone of the letter was less than pleasant. In fact, I would characterize it as business bullying. What this person didn't realize is that I save everything and I live for accountability. I have every email receipt, contract negotiation, and record of every transaction my business is involved with.

One of the accusations in the email was that I didn't actively participate in the approval process, and it had been compromised because of this. In reality, I had sat through many meetings, and had done at least ten times more work with this partner than any other partner I've been involved with. I cannot babysit design and manufacturing. Their process was also cumbersome and hard to manage. When we told them this, it seemed to fall on deaf ears. I had also rejected many of the ideas, but wanted to be clear that I do not reject things casually, but thoughtfully—and if the right people from the partner had been there to see what was being offered, they would likely have agreed with my decisions. We weren't getting anywhere, and yes, we were all frustrated, but you do not make progress on an issue like this with bullying tactics. Not with me you don't.

Before I responded to the email, I spent time clarifying and correcting every single point made in it. I also needed to address the tone of the letter, because I never want to receive something like that again, and I do not want anyone on my team to receive this kind of treatment.

I have walked away from potentially lucrative partnerships and millions of dollars because of a culture that I didn't appreciate or because of the way my staff or I was treated. If something doesn't work culturally for me, I won't do it financially. There is no amount of money you could pay me to work with people who have a negative and toxic work culture. I understand that not everybody has the financial means to do that, and I consider myself lucky, but you can find a way to reject poor behavior. In my experience a negative culture leads to many problems—poor morale, corner cutting, hostility, and low productivity, to name a few. And research backs me up. Never accept anything less than you deserve.

I didn't scorch the earth. I took a deep breath, crowdsourced with some trusted associates for advice about my response, assembled all the facts related to what was in the message, and wrote a professional, straightforward, unemotional email laying out all the inaccuracies that were in the email we had received. I stood my ground. After that, I reminded the partner that I am intimately involved in my brand. After all, I did not get on the cover of *Forbes* magazine by sleeping through meetings.

I also called another former partner in the same space to check in, and they told me they regretted letting me go and would take me back as a partner in a minute. They underscored for me that it is the name behind the product who has the leverage, not the company who makes the product. Of course, the manufacturer is important, but they need the name brand. I also called my distributor, and they assured me that they did not care who made the product, as long as the final result met my standards. Bingo. Now I knew when I wrote my email that if the partner didn't think the situation was a good fit, I was more than happy to fulfill all my existing obligations and, if necessary, I could walk away. I could go right back to my old partners. As I have said, I don't bluff. When I say something, I mean it. I walked away from the *Housewives* and MGM, leaving millions on the table. I do not fuck around.

Always find your power before you respond to an accusation or mistreatment. When a person bullies you in business, the person being bullied often feels that they have to back down because the other person is making such an aggressive power play. It can feel intimidating. In this situation, I did at first think that these partners were paying me a great deal of money so that gave them all the power and all the leverage. That's when I reached out to a variety of people in the industry to ask them about who has the leverage in such a situation. Part of my personal leverage is that there's no amount of money that will make me do something that doesn't make me feel good about myself. But I did want to find out where the pressure points were. Who's valuable in this partnership, them or me? I felt confident about ending my reply with a professional statement: If this relationship isn't working for you, I will honor all of my commitments, and I will gladly walk away, because I don't want to ever be involved in something that isn't working for me culturally.

We all have more power than we think. We absolutely have the power to subtly and methodically reject bad behavior. I give my assistant tools for this. For instance, if a partner or associate calls with a last-minute request for a meeting, I tell them to, in a nice way, thank the person and say something like, "This is so important and we are committed to this partnership, and had we not gotten only two days' notice we could have made it work. Here is timing that does work." In other words, kill them with kindness, make your point, and offer a solution.

Can you walk away from a bad situation if conditions do not improve? You probably can. You can't do it without talking to trusted advisors who can tell you whether you are evaluating the situation correctly. Everybody has leverage. You just have to look at the situation, evaluate your strengths, and be clear about the balance of power. Get those ducks in a row before you respond. Even a big company may not necessarily have the right to fire you without cause. It certainly does not have the right to bully or abuse you.

The person who wrote the letter quickly responded to me that the company absolutely wanted to continue the relationship. I got on the phone with them, and they began by talking about the process, the business, and the product. And I said, "You know, I am not worried about the process, the business, and the product. I know I can get those things done. I care about the culture." Once they understood that, they claimed that it was all a misunderstanding. I knew it wasn't, because one of my assistants had told me that every time she talked to this person, the conversation felt bullying and intimidating. I can only hope this experience taught the partner something about how behavior affects others, destroys processes, and hurts business. We are never too experienced or too high up in the chain of command to learn some humility.

I also called the head honcho, the main person in the partner company, and told them clearly and calmly that there would be no circumstances under which my team or I will ever accept an email like that from anyone ever. I repeated that if they didn't want to work with me, it was absolutely fine. I reiterated that I would fulfill my obligations and leave because I care much more about culture than money. This person assured me that they wanted to continue the relationship, and communication would be kept professional and friendly. I expect them to honor that promise going forward.

There is a happy ending. While we are still working through challenges, the air is clear and I am moving forward with this important partner.

Don't let bad behavior from others fester and grow. Never let anyone believe they can treat you badly. In

> **We all have more power than we think. Stand your ground.**

those terms, you *do* hold all the cards. Play them by laying down the law: treat me with respect.

B SMART

Push, Meet, Shove: The Don't-Fuck-with-Me Cheat Sheet

The truth is, bosses, colleagues, friends, romantic partners, and yes, even complete strangers can and do take advantage of us. It's human nature. If you're a people pleaser, you can find yourself in a precarious position when the demands people make on you pile up, especially if you don't know how to say no politely and firmly. Your good nature and natural inclination to give people the benefit of the doubt can also hurt you when dishonest people look for a target to swoop in on. It doesn't have to be this way. Here are three practical ways to build your reputation as a good person, but one who isn't a pushover.

1. *Tell the truth about where you're at.* Not long ago, I was asked to do a TV show in Los Angeles. Before I could say yes, I had to sit and look carefully at my calendar, including all my business commitments, events involving my daughter or her school, everything! The reason moms get burned out is that they are not organized, even though they are doing everything: working, running the house, making dinner, grocery shopping, and so on. No one works harder than a mother without help. You have to sit down with your kids and your spouse or partner, friends, and family to discuss schedules and chores. Be up front. No one can magically or psychically understand where you're at in terms of your time, interest, and needs, whether that's at home or at work. Don't wait until you have a major meltdown and blindside everyone with an unexpected blowup. Before that happens, learn to say what you need and feel, as in, "I need help with the laundry" or "Can you take the dog for a walk tonight?" or "I need extra time to finish this report" or "Are you able to give me some input on sales projections?" News flash: no one is going to stop loving you because you can't do everything. If someone does turn their back on you because you can't take their kid to gymnastics, maybe you just found out they weren't your friend in the first place. If your colleague at work isn't carrying their weight when you're both supposed to be working on a project, it may be time to document their shortfalls and talk to them about it before going to the boss (and know that you might have to do that too). Being true to yourself may be worth losing a few relationships in exchange for your self-worth.

2. *Don't devalue your time and skills.* If you create value and are working hard at something and not being rewarded for it the way you feel you should be, ask for the appropriate recognition or walk away. Think about other ways to get to the level

you want to reach, if it's not happening where you are at the present time. There's a good chance that you have many other talents that will be appreciated by someone who will match your value with the right money or work circumstances or environment. It's up to you to find it.

3. *If you've been taken advantage of, ripped off, or scammed, don't stay silent.* Be clear and set boundaries. Tell someone who can help. Keep at it until your problem gets the attention it deserves. Remember, if you allow someone to get away with doing a wrong, you are enabling them to do it again. When you speak up and pursue every avenue to make something right, you are not just seeking justice for yourself, you are helping other victims, and you're preventing future crimes and scams. If someone stabs you in the back at work, for instance, take my advice and address the wrongdoing clearly and with facts. Defend yourself. Hold them accountable by calling them on it. Sometimes it is necessary to go over their heads and talk to your boss—but do so only after you have your ducks in a row.

Pros Play Hurt

Both my daughter and I had COVID, and it was everything the medical professionals said it would be and more: miserable. My teeth were chattering, I had a fever and searing headaches, I was exhausted, my muscles ached, and there were days when I couldn't move. Both Bryn and I were tested at the first signs of not feeling well, around Christmas 2020. We were able to get tested every couple of days after that,

> Stay on the road, running at the pace that is right for you.

to monitor the virus's progression. While I was sick, I was still tending to Bryn, who was not hit as hard as I was, thank goodness. She also recovered much more quickly than I did. She is a strong, healthy girl.

COVID was brutal. Each day I thought I would get better, but I didn't feel as if I was getting better until one day when I felt better. It was like a switch. I got through the illness, and thank goodness I didn't have to be hospitalized or intubated.

During the time I was dealing with COVID, my business was still up and running. Products were being sold, deals were being made, employees were working. *Yes*, you should take care of yourself (which is why I make such a big deal about eating well, drinking enough water, moving your body, and getting enough sleep), and yes, when you are sick you need to get medical attention. But you can't always stop the presses. Even though there were days when I was sick and would lie in bed staring at the ceiling, I knew I had a child to mother, a business to run, employees to pay, dogs to walk. Sometimes you have to put on the big girl pants and get it done no matter what, because pros play hurt.

In the midst of feeling like death, I was asked to do a cocktail-related social media post for one of my partners. I wanted to do the post because it was good money; unfortunately, it had been scheduled before I became sick. Bryn had recovered completely by the time the date for the post rolled around, which was a blessing. My business manager told me we could not push off the opportunity for much longer; we either had to do it now or not do it. We were going to do it.

The problem was, no one could come in my house while I had COVID. My entire staff was working remotely. There was no way we could have the liability; I wouldn't do that to my staff even if one of them had volunteered to help. The other issue was that I didn't know how to set anything up to create the post, and I was still sick. The night before the shoot I asked Bryn if she thought she could set up the kitchen to do the shoot. She said yes, she thought she could. My then ten-year-old daughter called our social media person the morning of the shoot, who walked her through the setup over FaceTime. She followed directions and cut up the limes and lemons and set up the condiments and the tripod. I got myself out of bed, composed myself, got dressed, did minimal hair and makeup, and was able to get through the filming. The post was made. We did it!

Many years before that, I was on a book tour while pregnant with Bryn. It was one of those twelve cities in twenty-one days or maybe twenty-one cities in twelve days marathons. It's all a blur! Let's just say it was a lot of cities and a lot of bookstore signing events that had to be accomplished within a short time frame... while pregnant.

Finally, on the last day of the tour, I found myself at a bookstore in the Mall of America in Bloomington, Minnesota. This is the largest and most imposing shopping mall in the United States. Hundreds of people were standing in line eager to meet me, say hello, and have me sign the book they had just purchased at the bookstore. I looked at the line that had formed, which was snaking out the door of the bookstore and into the mall itself. It seemed endless to me, as if the entire population of Minnesota had shown up to meet me, bless their hearts.

I'm a warrior. I was also tired and bloated. But I just kept going, one foot in front of the other. You run the marathon one mile at a time. I took a deep breath and started the meet-and-greet. All I thought about was the person in front of me. When they walked away I thought about the next person who came up to the table where I sat. If I thought about the line, I might have gone into labor then and there. And if I had bagged the event, imagine the fallout. I had to get in the zone. I do not fold. I know where I come from. These people are precious. They represent all of the people, fans and followers, who have helped me succeed.

When the last book was signed, all I could think about was a long, hot bath. Molly, my assistant at the time, looked at me and said, "Dude, you're my hero." Maybe. But I'm also a pro running the marathon.

Is There a Doctor in the House?

My COVID experience also brought me face-to-face with another problem that tested my stamina: a scam; and I had to think of a way to resolve it that was discreet and fair. Because of my relief work during COVID, when I provided millions of N95 masks to first responders and others, I had good relationships with doctors and hospitals. My daughter and I had gone to a testing site and had been confirmed to have the virus. After that, I didn't want to go anywhere else and risk infecting other people. I wanted someone else to come here to do a second test and provide any needed care. I called my relief work partner and asked if he knew of any doctors in Connecticut who could make house calls. He sent a doctor to my house, who redid our COVID tests using rapid-result test kits.

The doctor ended up coming once a day on average for about eight days, and on a couple of occasions she came twice during the day. She administered the COVID rapid tests and checked on our general well-being. On a few occasions during that time, someone from her office came to my house to administer an IV to prevent dehydration.

The doctor was friendly. Once she brought us pastries, and she was in general competent and caring. Once COVID set in, I was down for the count. I felt like I was dying. It was Christmastime, and I so wanted to give Bryn a great holiday. We couldn't leave the house; we couldn't do much of anything while we were sick. When we were fully recovered, we went to the supermarket together to find ingredients for meals we wanted to prepare. It was a terrible time in many ways, but also a deeply memorable and meaningful one. We cooked together, watched movies, talked, and laughed. To this day, I can't make a bowl of ramen or pasta without thinking of my daughter. The beginning of the shutdown, and then living through COVID, made me understand how people feel in war and natural disaster–torn places, which I had been to many times in my relief work. People in those situations talk about how important faith and family are to survival, and COVID made me understand that in a personal way.

I also understood that if you're with your child, it doesn't matter if you're sitting in the last toilet bowl seat on an airplane or if you're home with COVID. You are with your most precious baby. I have fond memories of that time for that reason. It's time we shared and enjoyed and survived together. I will never get that time back, so I cherish it.

Once we had gotten negative COVID test results, Bryn and I traveled to Florida. When we were in Florida and before returning home, I had another rapid test done, and I was forty minutes late to the appointment. What I didn't realize at the time was that the person who administered this test was the Connecticut doctor's sister.

When I returned to Connecticut, I asked my staff if we had received a bill or gotten any information about the cost of the care and home visits we had received. Nothing. Months passed, and I kept asking if I could get a bill for the care. I wanted to see the bill and pay it. We had seen the doctor about ten times, and each time she spent about ten to fifteen minutes with us. It had to have cost something. Finally, the doctor sent her bill to my business manager.

It was $40,000. A shocking number. That represents an average year's salary.

I called my business manager to ask what the fuck was going on and requested he obtain an itemized bill. The doctor would not talk to my business manager because of the Health Insurance Portability and Accountability Act (HIPAA) rules, which protect medical information. I gave the doctor written permission to talk to my manager about the bill, and she finally sent an itemization of the costs. None of them made any sense to me.

The situation led to stress and anxiety. I know that I am a successful person. I am wealthy. I understand that. But this was an unreasonable amount of money. It was absolutely inflated and fraudulent. *It was wrong.* I had a mobile doctor who charged $350 for a visit during non-pandemic times, so even if the price was twice that, the total cost would have been $700 times ten visits, which would be $7,000. Still a significant amount of money, but nowhere near $40,000!

I had the number of a *New York Times* journalist whom I had talked to about a PPE scandal that had been uncovered while I was doing COVID relief work trying to get medical supplies out to first responders and others who needed them. Jack Nicas was delightful, an excellent reporter who had been instrumental in uncovering a Facebook scam among others, something he specializes in investigating. Meanwhile, my business manager had told me about another price gouging scam in Connecticut involving a Greenwich doctor. Jack told me about another reporter who had written an article about that Greenwich doctor. I reached out to the reporter and showed her the bills I had received from my doctor, along with all the information I had about the visits, how long they lasted, and what had happened during the time we had COVID.

The reporter said to me that it was the single most egregious instance of price gouging she'd ever seen. She looked at the doctor's website and saw some strange claims as well, that she was using a special proprietary technology and a faster rapid test than any other rapid testing.

What was I going to do? I knew I was being scammed, and I didn't want to pay someone $40,000 to keep them from going to the press to say I was a deadbeat. The last thing I want to be is a person who stiffs someone. I pay my bills. I talked to my business manager, and we decided to proactively send her a check to cover $1,000 for every visit, which is still overpaying for basic house calls. Combined with the visits for the IV, we wrote a check for $12,000.

As of this writing, the check I sent has never been cashed. I still lie awake wondering about it. I will never accept that the care I received was worth $40,000, especially since the doctor time and again refused to discuss or be transparent about the costs of the service she had agreed to provide.

Of course, you always have to be careful to avoid being a victim of a scam and scammers. Scams happen all the time and often to the smartest people. Virgin Group founder and mega-entrepreneur Richard Branson was nearly scammed out of $5 million when someone representing themselves as Britain's defense minister, Sir Michael Fallon, contacted him asking for financial help to secure the release of a diplomat being held by terrorists. He almost fell for it; the scammer was *that* good. Luckily, he did some research before releasing the funds and uncovered the crime.

This is to say that scammers are often pros; it's how they make their living. Never feel guilty or stupid if you are caught up in a scam. If you don't think like a criminal, you don't assume people are out to steal from you.

Life and business are exciting because we don't know what will happen next—and scary for the same reason. That's because you cannot predict everything that will happen—a nasty email comes out of nowhere, a pandemic hits, someone treats you badly when you least expect it, something happens to your health or life that temporarily derails you, someone else may try to take advantage of you when you thought you had all your I's dotted and T's crossed. In closing out this chapter, I want to encourage you to just stay on the road, running at the pace that is right for you, with the knowledge that you're moving forward. Keep your eyes open, and be productive and proactive. Focus on what you want to accomplish, and solve problems with thought but do so as they happen. Don't get jammed up, and you will get where you want to go.

10

Protect the Realm

THE NAME OF THIS BOOK IS *BUSINESS IS PERSONAL* (AND THE PER-
sonal is business) because I believe it, and I live it. My two brands,
Skinnygirl and Bethenny, are completely intertwined with my life,
which is why it's so important to protect not just my "brand" but
the entire realm—my reputation and integrity, my business and
brands, and my partners and employees. Skinnygirl was a brand
I created in my thirties that reflected a lighter and more carefree
coming-of-age woman than Bethenny, which is more elevated.
I created it to reflect the woman I have become: a sophisticated
working mother and philanthropist who is interested in quality
over quantity.

When one of my products hits the market, whether it's a television show, a pair of jeans, sunglasses, popcorn, or whatever I
come up with in the future, it has to represent me, who I am as a
person, and what I stand for. I am known as someone who does
not promote anything I would not use myself. Slapping my name

on anything without ensuring it meets my standards will cause my brand to deteriorate over time. I don't take a smash-and-grab approach; I want my efforts to have lasting value. Authenticity and quality are core values of the realm. My customers expect nothing less, and they shouldn't. People have to be confident that I will always fulfill my promise to deliver excellence every time. If I don't, it doesn't just hurt my brand, it hurts my customers, and it hurts me. This standard also means there will be times when hard decisions are necessary.

Years ago, I did a line of deli meats under the Skinnygirl name. It made sense in a way; deli meats are generally jammed with nitrates, loads of salt, and other unhealthy ingredients. The Skinnygirl version was lighter and somewhat better. They were sold at Walmart. But ultimately, the meats didn't reflect who I truly am (I often eat a vegan diet) and what Skinnygirl was meant to be. I don't eat deli meats often, and I don't buy them. I just felt weird about the product line. My agents at the time pushed me because they wanted a deal with Walmart. Offers to partner that don't feel exactly right still come to me today, but I have much more discretion and discipline about what kind of partnerships I form. I'm strict and I hold the line. It's not about the money, and money is the wrong reason to do anything in business. You can get lost, and quickly.

For instance, I've stuck to my principle of booking only the most amazing people on my podcast, which is a big part of protecting my realm, the show itself, and frankly, the people who have appeared on it and whom I hope to book in the future. If I booked one clown, someone who isn't serious or hasn't done something truly innovative and succeeded at it (and my original podcasting partners pitched us a lot of clowns), the show's integrity would be compromised. One terrible guest would belittle all the other smart, thoughtful, and badass guests I've had on.

One guest pitch we received was for a person who was the sibling of a very well-known person but who was known in her own right as a stoner with a social media following. That's not enough. I thought, no, this person would be an insult to the fine guests who have been gracious enough to come on my podcast. What has she done on her own? What defines her as a mogul? Nothing. We have a strong filter to determine who makes an amazing guest and offers real value to listeners. They have to have created something recognizable and demonstrate sustained success.

If you have a brand that is precious and good, you can cheapen it quickly by agreeing to work with or include less than stellar "ingredients"—whether that be a person, product, or partner. Successful people across the board operate though this same lens. I want to share what super chef and restaurateur Wolfgang Puck told me about protecting the realm—he's the right person to talk about it because high-end, fine dining restaurants make a promise to customers that they will give them food that is consistently good every time. Protecting the realm in this and all businesses is about *quality control.*

When Wolfgang Puck expands his realm by opening restaurants around the world, he makes sure to sign management deals and not licensing deals, because that gives him more control over the quality of the food and the management of the business. So fascinating. "I have run my business successfully for forty years," he told me. "I do not want to work for anybody because I love what I do. I don't want anyone to tell me that I have to lower my food costs by buying frozen shrimp, or lower quality beef, or produce that isn't fresh from the farmer's market. I want to run the business the way I see it."

When he signs a management agreement with an investor to open a Spago, it means his company controls 100 percent of the

way the restaurant is run, whether it
is in Istanbul, Budapest, Los Angeles,
or Singapore. "The people who work
in those restaurants are our chefs, our
managers, and our responsibility."

> Authenticity and
> quality are core
> values of the realm.

That's the way to protect the realm: by keeping control of what is
important, the quality of your results.

Dangerous Waters

My recent foray into swimsuit design and manufacturing is a perfect example of the importance of quality over quantity, and truth
over money. The story not only defines who I am as a person but it
also demonstrates that doing the right thing can be difficult, but in
the long run, it is always the better choice and, frankly, easier than
dealing with the aftermath of doing the wrong thing.

I have a successful shapewear line under Skinnygirl that
helps women of all shapes and sizes look and feel better in their
clothes. Shapewear was the first product line I did after cocktails.
It represents my longest and most profitable partnership. Today,
the products sell without a substantial effort on my part because
they're well-priced and high quality and have a proven track record
with customers. I trust my partner to create a product that solves a
problem for women, which is to shape them in a comfortable and
not overly confining way, which in turn makes their clothing fit
and look better. They are streamlined with no tricked-out gadgets
or extras, but simply a good first layer for your body. The products
have helped women breastfeed; they've helped women who have
had breast cancer. They cater to women who have small breasts,

and those who have large breasts. Skinnygirl shapewear is a practical solution that's also true to the brand.

Flash forward several years, and I started to think about swimwear. It's another great category that is related to shapewear, and for that and other reasons I've always wanted to be involved with it. First of all, I love the ocean and a beach walk so I wear a lot of swimsuits. In fact, when I am photographed I am often in a bathing suit. I look fairly decent in a bathing suit (for my age). With the blossoming of social media and interest in the private lives of well-known people, I am photographed, unfiltered, when I am out in public. I have also posted photos of myself in a bathing suit on my own social media accounts.

When I looked at photos of me in a bathing suit, it occurred to me that many brands were getting credit for what I was wearing, meaning if I was photographed wearing a brand I personally liked, it looked like I was endorsing it. And I am absolutely advertising it when wearing it, which is why swimsuit companies have sent us swimsuits over the years. But I wasn't being paid for those endorsements. This led me to think about having my own line of swimwear. It's something I've long wanted to do, as I said, and maybe the timing was right. The swimwear could incorporate the shapewear technology we had already developed, which would solve a practical problem for women looking for something flattering to wear at the beach or the pool. It's so stressful for most women to find a nice-looking bathing suit that gives them a sense of confidence and comfort.

For this line, I wanted to do something high end and beautiful with great lines and draping; sophisticated, minimalist, shaping, and super flattering (of course!). It would be affordable luxury: well-made and well-priced. Those were my promises—and yes, I knew they were big. I partnered with a well-known company known for high-end resort clothing and swimwear as a way of guaranteeing the end product would achieve the quality and style I expected.

Another important part of creating a successful line was branding it properly. Skinnygirl might seem like a natural choice, but in my mind it wasn't. I didn't want to do the swimwear line under the Skinnygirl label for a couple of reasons. First, even though Skinnygirl makes clothing and shapewear for all women and it is absolutely size inclusive, swimwear is one of the most anxiety-producing purchases women make. While the term Skinnygirl connects well to other products I make, including lower fat and lower calorie popcorn, salad dressing, and better-for-you preserves, and potentially, my supplements, I felt it would be off-putting for swimwear. My brand Bethenny felt like better branding for this swimwear line. I wanted the line to appeal to a more mature woman, and to all women whose bodies show the badges of PMS, pregnancy, menopause, and so on. Frankly, I also had concerns around cancel culture, and being called out for using words (both "skinny" and "girl") that bring a lot of women anxiety on top of the emotion around finding a bathing suit that is flattering, especially if you are older, and if you're curvy. In fact, Skinnygirl is intentionally one word to create a new concept around an attitude. My customers come in all beautiful shapes and sizes. I saw what happened when Victoria's Secret came under fire for its branding and exclusive use of thin and tall models. I certainly didn't want to be in a position to have to change branding midstream because Skinnygirl swimsuits backfired because of the wrong branding. It would be tough to recover from that—not impossible, but not easy either.

The Bethenny line is elevated stylistically, which is what I wanted for the bathing suits. Skinnygirl is a great brand, but it's meant to be casual and fun, not overly sophisticated. However, we are looking into more high-end products for Skinnygirl, so the option to include luxury under the name is always open. I wanted my swimwear to be reminiscent of or in the tradition of Donna Karan, Norma Kamali, and ERES: elegant, sophisticated, and high quality. It made sense. Understandably, HSN wanted to put the line under Skinnygirl because it was a proven name that our customers were familiar with and trusted. What happens at a place like HSN is that you build an audience based on your brand, and those customers become loyal to the brand. HSN would have effectively been starting a new brand with the Bethenny line. Their swimwear manufacturing partner also wanted to do it under the Skinnygirl label for the same reasons: it was a known entity.

These suits had sleek and beautiful silhouettes, elegant, classic, and chic. They are not about tie-dye, distressing, ripping, being brazenly sexy, or being age-inappropriate. I simply did not feel that the line should be called Skinnygirl. I kept pushing both HSN and the manufacturing partner. It was getting late in the game, but I felt it would be worth it for the branding to match what the swimsuits were supposed to be. I persisted and insisted. We went back and forth about the name. My gut instinct was too strong on this one.

I got past that hurdle, and the line would be under the Bethenny label. Great! I was excited to be moving forward with HSN, an incredible partner.

Two weeks before the suits would go on sale at HSN, we did some pre-launch social media, and I noticed some issues with the suits. This was the first time I had seen the product in person; I had not received any actual samples of fabric or prototypes at this point. Because of the COVID pandemic, the approval process had all been done via Zoom meetings. At the prior Zoom meeting,

I noticed problems on the models with the fit of the suits. Even through the screen I could see problems with the design and fit, had pointed them out, and was told they would be and then had been corrected. When I saw them on the day of the pre-launch Instagram post, those issues still hadn't been resolved.

As I held one of the suits in my hand, I noticed that the fabric felt thick. I tried it on and, whoa, my boobs popped out of the size medium, as if it were a size extra-extra-small—and I'm a small person. I told my COO that I didn't like the way the suit looked or fit. Something was wrong with the cut and design. Although I am small, I am usually a good indicator of fit because I am true to size and an off-the-rack shopper. I have bought bathing suits at a drug-store in a pinch for nine dollars, they fit me, and I've happily worn them. My COO took a video of how the suit fit me and sent it to our manufacturing partner. The bigger problem? The full product run had already been made and delivered. There wasn't anything we could do about the actual swimsuits.

I reviewed the virtual approval process in my mind, and considered a different scenario had they sent me samples earlier, before the actual manufacturing had started. Maybe I could have stopped production and made changes had I received prototypes much earlier. But I'm just one person. I certainly don't reflect every woman's body. We still could have had the same problem even if a sample suit had fit me well, and likely would have since I would have had to receive a prototype of every suit style in every size we offered. I would have had to arrange for a variety of women to try them on, which is probably what should have happened, but it didn't.

Sometimes but not always, clothing manufacturers use a standard fit model, generally a size 8, and then produce sizes larger and smaller using dimensions based on that size. Other times they use standard sizing calculations, which is why major mass marketed brands are similar in terms of how they are sized. That's why I can buy the same size bathing suit in most department stores (or a Walgreens) and I know it will fit me even if I can't try it on. I had to deal with the problem in front of me: badly designed and manufactured swimsuits that did not represent my vision, my brand, my expectations, or those of my customers. For now, I'd wait to hear back from our partners.

What could have been done differently? After the first Zoom meeting, when I mentioned that the material looked too thick, I did ask the partner and manufacturing representative if they could assure me that the mistakes would and could be corrected. But even if I had made the point more strongly, at that stage I don't think there would have been anything that could have been done. Perhaps my COO Jill could have been more forceful about our concerns. Perhaps I would have felt better if we had stated our concerns and displeasure more strongly. But we *had* aired our doubts. There is not much room for error in the fit of a swimsuit. There's some leeway with sizing in a sweatshirt or a loose blouse, but the cut of swimsuits has to be precise. We also can't underestimate the customer—she is a savvy buyer who wants quality and fashion at a good price. I don't want to insult the intelligence of my smart and thoughtful customers.

After our manufacturing partners received the visuals from us, they responded by saying that the bathing suits were made with compression fabric similar to shapewear, so of course it was going to be a tight fit. We make shapewear with compression fabric, and it's not as thick or bulky as the swimwear fabric. The straps on the suits were bulky and ill-fitting. While the partner and the manufacturer had both worked with curvy girl sizes, they were not the focus of their businesses. I had told the partner that we needed larger sizes. Now they were under the impression that we were doing a "plus size line," which they had no experience with. It was not a plus size line, and I reject that term; I don't like it. We simply needed larger sizes that were cut properly, to serve our curvy customers, and in sizes that were consistent with American women and consumer expectations. These suits met none of these expectations.

Yes, I was freaking out. There was no way I was going to put my name on a terrible product and sell it to women! We make quality clothes that are comfortable and fit well. Everybody who buys our jeans, shapewear, casual dresses, tops, and bottoms loves them. Those same customers expect the same great experience with any new apparel product I introduce. I want them to have a great experience too—I do not want to let any of my fans, followers, or customers down. They are always top of mind in my businesses. I am also known for not doing or selling anything I do not believe in. That is my business *and* my personal philosophy. Allowing these bathing suits to enter into the marketplace would be a disaster on so many levels. It would compromise the trust of my customers that I have worked hard to achieve.

We were scheduled to do an Instagram Live at five o'clock in the afternoon to talk about the suits. I had little time to get ready—a matter of minutes. We had already had a crazy day of shooting other things, aside from preparing to launch a swim line that was not up to standards. Making matters more complicated, I had been interviewed for an article about the line that appeared in *Women's Wear Daily*, the fashion industry's bible, on launch day.

I tried putting on a different bathing suit that I had tried on a couple of weeks earlier, hoping it would fit better, but it too was all wrong. It was not molding to my body. The bodice was way out in front of me like a shelf, and gigantic to boot. The suit felt bulky and uncomfortable. The straps were too thick and rounded, not flat and sleek. It just didn't feel good. The bathing suits were supposed to make the wearer feel beautiful, comfortable, and chic. They were supposed to flatter the figure. I tried on another suit, and I was popping out of the top and bottom as with the earlier sample, even though it was one size larger than I normally wear! Even if I planned on selling only to small people, and what would be the point of that, these suits still wouldn't work.

Then I looked at all the other samples. We were four minutes out from the Instagram Live at that point. I asked everybody on my staff who was in my house, including my COO and my assistant, to choose a suit in their size and try it on. We all represent different ages, body types, and sizes, so we were a broad-spectrum case study. Every single one of us looked terrible in these suits. One of my assistants is still traumatized by the suit—I don't think she's put on a bathing suit since! They made all of our bodies look bad. None of us felt good about ourselves. I could not and would not sell these suits.

Of course, at that point everyone—my business manager, partners, and others—were saying to me, what the fuck, Bethenny. This represented hundreds of thousands of dollars' worth of merchandise sales. HSN is expecting to sell this. Even my business manager fought me on it. "You should have said something two weeks ago," he said. We *had* said something. Jill, my COO, had sent the video recording the flaws two weeks earlier. At that point the window was already closed. The problems couldn't have been corrected because the inventory had been produced and packaged.

I could not go on social media and talk about these suits with any level of sincerity, unless of course it was to tell viewers how crappy they were, which is something I wasn't going to do either. "I don't care," I said to my business manager. "I'm not promoting them on Instagram. And I am not going to sell them on HSN." He freaked out, which I understood, but I also wasn't budging. When the time came, I put on Skinnygirl jeans and started selling my Bethenny glasses. I just started talking about other things—good thing I can talk on the fly.

The tech crapped out and the Instagram Live was a disaster. Even though I've been doing this a while, it was a shit show. Everything was happening so quickly, I started to wonder whether this Instagram Live was on my own feed or being filmed on the HSN Instagram feed. Because I was cursing about the tech failure... and I was worried because if I was on HSN I'd get canceled pretty quickly for doing that. It was my feed, so that was good. I collected myself and told the audience that someday I would tell them the bathing suit story. For now, I wanted to reassure them that I do not endorse anything I don't believe in. I explained that we had just had a behind-the-scenes disaster and ten things had gone wrong. After the Instagram Live was over, my assistant said the only thing that hadn't happened that day was me appearing naked on social media—which, trust me, might have been an option in some of those suits.

After the Instagram Live ended, I got on the phone to the head of HSN apparel. My business manager at the time had asked me not to call her, afraid I would hurt the relationship with HSN if I told her the swimsuits could not be sold. I didn't listen, because I knew a leader would want to know all the details of a situation like this one. I operate from a place of truth, not fear. I was also thinking about the massive number of customer returns HSN would receive, the bad online reviews, and customer complaints aired on social media—and *all* of it would be justified. I made the call and told the HSN executive the whole story, including about the badly made samples, my request for changes, and about our experience trying on the suits. "I don't think it is a good product. I can't sell it. HSN shouldn't sell it," I said. Maybe telling her this would hurt me with HSN, but selling the suits would hurt *all* of us so much more. I was willing to take a hit with HSN if I had to, because I knew I was right. I was protecting the brand and myself but I was also protecting HSN. If you sell a bad product it will cost so much more in the long run than potentially taking a loss by putting a stop to the sale.

The HSN executive listened quietly, and then said, "One hundred percent, you're right. You can't sell something you don't believe in." Okay, I got through that. The next morning, my business manager called to tell me that the partner who made the bathing suits was freaking out. "This is going to be a lawsuit, they're going to get the lawyers," he told me. "You should have said two weeks ago, stop the press." I thought that was bullshit, because first, we did indicate problems during the production phase, and even if we had received the suits two weeks earlier, there wouldn't have been much anyone could have done about it at that point.

The partner said that they had fixed the suit, but they had only fixed the suit for a size zero. I know my size, but I don't know what it's going to be like for all the other sizes, so it was a good thing that I just happened to ask other women to try them on, and that they all felt the same way I did. They all agreed that the suits made them look and feel terrible. They did not fit correctly. Still, my business manager insisted I was going to be sued. I said that I didn't care, let them sue me. If I sent these suits to one of the main investors in the manufacturing company, whom I knew, he would say the same thing I did, that the product was shit. There was no way anyone with any knowledge of bathing suit construction would assess these products as good to go. The flaws were not minor.

At this point, the discussion was getting heated. My business manager and I were yelling at each other. It's not fun to be Monday morning quarterbacking. I said, look, we can't launch this line with the product we have. It didn't matter what the contract said. The suits were unacceptable. We can be in real life or we can be in fantasy land, but I was not going to sell shit, and I didn't care if I had to pay for it, because I was not going to ruin my brand. This was high stakes poker now, working with multi-billion-dollar partners, including HSN. I told my business manager about the process that goes on at HSN: they receive garments and they have to look at them to ensure they fit various shapes and sizes and body types. But HSN also sells thousands of SKUs (stock keeping unit, or inventory) a day, which means that it's impractical and not possible for them to do an entire fitting of every individual item for every brand.

> If you sell a bad product it will cost so much more in the long run than potentially taking a loss by putting a stop to the sale.

HSN could not be blamed for this debacle at all. Swimwear was something new for them and for me. HSN should not have to pay for the goods; I would eat it if I had to. I introduced them to the partner, so it was on me. I had to own it. This represented tens of thousands of dollars, so it was not an insubstantial sum of money. But I agreed: they should not have to pay for the unacceptable inventory.

My business manager said that my partner was now going to take the inventory and sell it to lower-price department stores. Every company in the apparel industry has a deal that says whatever they don't sell in regular stores can go to stores like JCPenney, Marshalls, and T.J. Maxx. I have no problem with those stores. I shop at those stores; I love those stores—I live at those stores! The problem is, those stores sell good products. My name would still be on the suits, and I didn't think they should be sold at outlet stores. When someone buys something, whether it's at Walgreens for $9 or Neiman's for $2,000, it should fit properly.

Now I had a new problem, because not only did I not want to sell these suits at HSN, I didn't think they should be sold period. They should not be on the open market at all. I had an idea. I said to my business manager, "This is how we handle this properly. Let's get the product on the HSN models, who represent all shapes and sizes, because HSN sells clothing to all women. I want to see this product on a bunch of people. If everybody says, Bethenny, you're crazy, these suits are great, I'll concede the argument," I said. "If the models try them on, and they feel great and say wow, this is a great product, we should be selling this, I will go out tomorrow and I'll sell all of them." Who knows, maybe all the suits we received as samples were a fluke, and the bulk of the inventory was in line with my expectations. I was more than willing to find out.

My business manager agreed to ask HSN about getting some of their models to try on the suits—I was hoping they'd give the green light because I wanted to resolve the issue, and I needed to start sleeping again. It's a hard space to be in because I have to be able to stand behind the product, but I am not a technical designer, and I am not an engineer. I can't be the talent, and the designer, and the approver, and deal with every single problem that comes up in the design and manufacturing of a product. I need to be able to trust my partners and their expertise in the areas of product development, design, and manufacturing. But at the end of the day, I know that if the suits are terrible, it's not the manufacturer who will be blamed, or HSN, or the swimsuit company that helped create the line. It's all on me. My name is on the product. I'm the one selling it; people are buying it because of me.

My business manager called me back a couple of days later to tell me I was going to be able to sleep that night. He had spoken to the head stylist at HSN, who told him that she had a problem with the product when it came in, but decided not to jump up and down about it because they were not experts on swim. They had relied on the expertise of the swim manufacturer, assuming that it knew what it was doing. HSN also sells thousands of units every five minutes; they don't have time to do granular analysis of individual items, as I said.

The HSN stylist told him, "Bethenny is a rock star. We could not have sold this product. In fact, the models did try the suits on and they didn't like them." Afterward, the people at HSN told me the models were actually applauding in the studio when they heard they didn't have to model the suits. Even they didn't want to walk out on television in them. And these models are not prima donnas; they are not the kind of people who say, oh, I'm not going to wear this or that. They are so professional and accommodating.

Ultimately, my company did pay for some of the suits, and some of the units were sold off in lots but in a way that did not compromise me or my brand. I am working with a new partner on a swimwear line, and I feel confident it will be the kind of product I can stand behind and that buyers will love.

There are a few morals to this story. First, you will often have an unpopular opinion, and it's hard to express it when no one is backing you up. But when something does not feel right in your stomach, your heart, and your mind, you've *got* to stand up and say something. It's the same with any business issue or a personal challenge. You could be breaking off an engagement or moving.

Years ago, I had gotten engaged, but something felt wrong about it. I didn't feel that it was the right thing to do, which became clearer to me as I began rationalizing my engagement, telling myself he was a nice guy and he'd be a great father. Ultimately, that didn't fly, because I knew in my heart and my gut and my mind that getting married to that, yes, nice guy at that time in my life was all wrong.

The more you delay doing what you know is right, the deeper you get in, and the harder it is to stop the train. If we had gone on HSN and tried to sell those suits, it would have been a disaster. We would have wasted an hour of HSN corporate and viewers' time. There would have been bad reviews and costly customer returns to deal with. Instead, I sold my clothes and glasses on my next HSN appearance, and we did quite well. I also maintained my integrity, and protected the realm, which includes all my partners and their brands, like HSN. I could sleep at night knowing I did the right thing.

Of course, problems like this are not always going to work out exactly the way you want them to. But this is the only person I can be, and it's the only person you can be if you want to walk with your head up. I called Kevin Huvane, co-chairman of the Creative Artists Agency, when it was all over, since I don't have parents to share these stories with. He's my consigliere, and I had to tell *someone* this crazy story. He said to me, "Bethenny, this is what makes you you. This is why you are successful, because if something doesn't feel right you don't let it slide." He continued, "I've done it myself, even when we were going to lose money on something; it's a business, and if we do it wrong, it's going to be a much bigger disaster." Sometimes the loss is worth it to protect the value and trust you've built. That's a precious thing, more valuable than the cost of thousands of crappy swimsuits.

B·SMART

In the Swim: Lessons Learned

Here's what bathing suits taught me about protecting the realm:

1. Make sure all your partners are on the same page as you are, and you're all working toward the same goal. And get it into your agreement with them—in writing.

2. When you enter into any new venture, one that is new to you, understand what's at stake. The small details matter. I should have gotten a swatch or material sample; I should have understood what size charts the manufacturer was using.

3. When something feels wrong, examine that feeling. Don't sweep it under the rug. I knew there was an issue with the bathing suits, and it wasn't just me or my body. I had to speak up.

4. Do the right thing because your reputation and integrity are on the line. Pretending everything is okay makes problems worse.

5. One small problem can get big quickly if it's not addressed immediately. As I have said, cracks become craters. Is it worth it?

6. Be willing to take a short-term loss if the product or idea is not executed correctly. Remember, you're in it to win it in the long haul.

You Are Alone in Your Decisions

Taking responsibility for your decisions is the core behavior for protecting the realm. At the end of the day, it's on you to decide how you want your business to run, what kind of quality you want to offer. It's up to you to take ownership of the decisions around your business. Yes, you can get advice, but the final answer must come from you, and you have to be right with it.

I have been making autonomous decisions that bucked popular opinion or the advice I was getting for a long time, and I have no plans on stopping now. You have to feel good about what you are doing, and sometimes you have to get away from the noise of other people and think things through on your own. Yes, you need the best information you can get, and you should seek knowledge from experts. But you are on your own when you say yes or no, this way or that way.

Protecting the realm is up to you. You can have people help and advise you, but only you can ensure the integrity of your brand, personal integrity, and personal dignity—those things are not up for grabs. Your ass is on the line. While you can't possibly know everything, you do have to take ownership of the decisions around what you do and whom you work with. That means knowing as much as you can and basing decisions on the best knowledge possible when decision time comes. This is why knowing the context is vital when making decisions. When someone asks me for a decision, whether it is around an event or a new product, I need to know the surrounding details. What is the event for? Who is sponsoring it, and how does it serve me and serve them? Is it relevant to my goals? For products, are we talking about an item that will sell thousands of units over time, or something seasonal and timely that will sell within a narrow window? The answers to those questions inform the call to attend the event or sign off on a product.

Making your own decisions also doesn't mean you have to *do* everything. I don't do my own corporate taxes, and I'd never represent myself in court. However, I also never assume anyone is smarter than I am, including accountants and lawyers. Ultimately, I am responsible for the decisions that concern my life and business. I'm on the hook, I'm the one who has to live with the decisions I make. That's why only I have the final say about the things that concern me. I ask questions, do research, look for insight from experts, but after all that data is compiled, what to do with it is all on me.

> The energy from walking away when your gut tells you to is so truthful that other good things come.

I know what I know, and I know what I don't know. If I am making decisions around financing or a deal structure, about actual money, I might go to my business managers and lawyers and listen to them. If it's about a creative way to do a deal and everyone in the room is stuck, and I'm having a battle back and forth, I can always figure it out if I give the issue some breathing room. I step back from the challenge when we're all jamming our head against the wall or if we're at an impasse, and then I can always break through; I usually can solve the problem when I understand it. Understand your business; don't let other people control its important parts. If I fundamentally go with my gut and decide out of truth I am not worried about the outcome of my decision, I will be right with it.

Earlier in the book I mentioned a wine deal I worked on. We were able to go far with the first people who had approached us about creating a branded wine. We had actually reached the signing stage of the negotiation. It would have been such an easy contract to fulfill, and I could have made a lot of money. But I didn't like the way the people working for the wine company spoke to my team. I didn't like the way it felt. And I walked. I had to deal with a major partner who was going to pay me high six figures a year just to stay in a partnership with few obligations on my part. Theoretically they would have paid me to take a nap, but that would not have been an act with any integrity. Integrity is what happens when no one is looking. Unfortunately, I didn't like their energy.

Just like the story I told in the last chapter, about the executive who had written a nasty email to my staff, I feel culture and attitude are so important when working with people. It's more important than the money because culture and values are lasting; money comes and goes. You can always make money. Some of the conflicts we were experiencing with the wine company felt extremely negative. Walking away from that was so freeing. It felt so right. The energy from walking away when your gut tells you to is so truthful that other good things come. You make room for better decisions when you aren't stuck in negative energy, and you receive a flow of new energy.

It's similar to what happened when I left the *Housewives*. I was alone in my decision to leave the show. I was also alone in my decision to go back to the *Housewives*, and I was alone in my decision to leave the show for the final time. I was on top of my game, and I was making more money than anyone in the franchise at the time. But the environment felt so toxic and negative. It was draining. Being on the show at that time made me feel dishonest. I didn't like that feeling, and I didn't want to continue under those circumstances. I had to decide on my own, out of truth. My business manager said I was leaving millions of dollars on the table. It's not that easy to make money like that. Someone else I know told me that trees grow high but they don't go to the sky—take the millions of dollars. That may be true, but what else would I do, what value could I add to the world, what money could I make, if I didn't have the *Housewives* hanging over my head?

Even though smart, successful people advised me to stay for another season, I said to myself, *I can make this happen. I can leave.* And by the way, I had to focus and motivate myself after I left to pursue other avenues of business and to build on what I had created apart from the *Housewives*. I couldn't just sit on my ass. I had to make sure that I could build new bridges. And that's what I did after I left the show: I made other decisions, created new products, developed another television show, started a podcast. Every decision was mine, and every one of them was made with the intent of expanding and protecting the realm.

The Skinnygirl brand all started with a ready-to-drink low-calorie margarita. When I was concocting it in my kitchen, I never imagined that it would turn into a broad line of product extensions, including shapewear and jeans. At that time, I was focused on creating a great tasting margarita that I didn't feel bad about drinking, and that I thought other women would like too. I didn't know I was naming a brand. But it did become a brand. When I decided to create a line of jeans under the Skinnygirl name, it had to be done with finesse, and it had to be inclusive. To address those issues, my brand partners and I were careful to explain that Skinnygirl jeans helped you unleash all of your inner Skinnygirl. The jeans represent a state of mind that's not about being thin. We had to overstate that idea and reinforce it every time we sold, marketed, or advertised the jeans. It's not about being a specific size or weight. The same is true of the other products under the Skinnygirl name. Everything under the brand reinforces that idea.

When I was developing a line of sunglasses, however, I knew that I wanted them to be under the Bethenny brand versus the Skinnygirl brand. This was part of an effort to find products that were sophisticated, glamorous, and high fashion, for women of discerning taste, and who had evolved, as I have, from youthful, single, and carefree, to more mature, working mothers, professional, philanthropic, and sophisticated. I had long known that the Bethenny brand would be reserved for products like fragrance, gorgeous sheets and towels, and beautifully scented candles that fit the Bethenny brand profile. Glam sunglasses fit perfectly into this profile and aesthetic. My decision to create the sunglass line under the Bethenny brand was the right one, even though, like the swimwear line, the branding met some resistance with my partners. I stood alone, but because I was right, others gathered when they saw it was the right decision.

Don't talk. Do. People talk too much, they tell people their idea, they tell people their process. They become desperate for other people to make decisions for them, and that never works. When you depend on others to make up your mind for you, you forget that people have agendas of their own. People can bring negative feelings, bad energy, and jealousy into their opinion process. This can be contagious, and can clutter your mind with extraneous ideas and opinions that cloud your own thinking.

It can be wise to solicit opinions during certain times, when you're in an open mode, before you've formed your own thoughts in a solid way; you need to collect data and information. But then you have to get into your own headspace, in your own zone. There's a point at which crowdsourcing opinions is counterproductive and harmful. Consensus is not necessary for the decisions that affect your bottom line, which are not just financial. The bottom line is anything that has a direct effect on your well-being, happiness, and success as a person.

You also don't need to explain everything to everybody and in the process get dragged down with negativity and naysayers. This doesn't mean you're not open-minded and that you don't hit roadblocks and ask for help. You may need some navigation at some point, but you need to monitor and manage it. You have to be conscious of who is giving you advice and why. If you start thinking about what everybody else is doing and saying, you're going to become confused and disheartened. At some point you need to say stop, I have enough information and now I need to be alone in my decision.

When you feel you have enough data, it's not like closing the door on further help. If I run into a problem, I can ask for help because there's always a network of others who have similar issues. What you don't need is to feel self-conscious about your decision-making process. Focus on your own game, and have the courage of your own convictions.

11

The Wolves at the End of the Bed

UNLESS THEY'RE NARCISSISTS OR DRINKING THEIR OWN KOOL-Aid, most people who achieve some level of success in business or life, and are recognized or celebrated for it whether within their social circle, locally, or nationally, are subject to insecurity. Do you deserve the success? You do, but you still end up feeling nervous about it, right? You can call this feeling the imposter syndrome, or the emperor has no clothes, or the too-good-to-be-true syndrome. You know the feeling. When everything is going well, you start to think it's just a matter of time before you fall on your face. You have this feeling when the stars seem to align in business and life. It makes for anxiety and discomfort. I'm not being negative, it's just gravity. I call it the wolves at the end of the bed—but they're all in our minds.

Yes, it is true that there are people who are jealous and waiting for you to fail, and enjoy it when you do. That was certainly a negative aspect of my experience on the *Housewives*. There was a definite element of satisfaction among the participants when one of the cast members got in trouble. There's a word for this: schadenfreude, which means deriving pleasure from another person's misfortune. It's the "I'm up here and you're down there" philosophy of life. Sad. It's also human nature, to a certain extent. But that doesn't matter—you can't control the thoughts and motivations of others. You can only control yourself, and how you interact with the world, online, and in real life in terms of whom you associate with. And that's what this chapter is about: managing your successes so that your failures don't destroy them.

When you are an entrepreneur, the wolves can often take the form of competitors. If you're well known in your field, or if your successes are recognized in your peer or professional group, the wolves can also be the watchers or the media (including local social media), which, while an incredible tool, is also always in search of a compelling story, especially if it's negative. Your friends, family, fans, and followers can turn into wolves if you start to think that you're above it all. Critics and fans alike are waiting and watching. And they might relish it if you fail. The wolves can hurt you and your business if you allow them to, especially if you forget that your life and your business aren't bulletproof.

While I was writing this book, I had a moment where I thought things were going *too* well, and it showed. In other words, my successes were public—I had a new show coming out and I was getting a lot of good press. My philanthropy, the B Strong Initiative, was achieving results through its needed relief work, raising $20 million for PPE products to distribute all over the country. My fear was that since there was so much corruption in the manufacturing and selling of masks to nonprofits during the pandemic, I would be caught in the middle of something bad in dealing with these corrupt people, a necessary evil when vetting aid.

Moreover, some people aren't comfortable with other people's success. Maybe it's because of jealousy or competitiveness, or because some people simply don't like them and they want to see them fail. I also know that at some point, something in my life or business *is* going to crash: a decision will be ill-conceived, the timing of a new idea might be off, mistakes will be made. I want to live in such a way that when a negative happens, it becomes an organic facet of building a business, creating a life, and being a human being. Because it is! What failures do *not* have to turn into are major business crises. We all have to deal with unsavory people at some point in our careers, so we have to figure out how to navigate that and keep our integrity intact. To keep the wolves at the end of the bed of your mind at bay, you need to do three important things: take care of yourself mentally and physically; don't believe your own hype; and don't go out of your way to make yourself vulnerable by creating an unrealistic public picture of your life and your work—stay humble and practice humility.

> You can't control the thoughts and motivations of others. You can only control yourself and how you interact with the world.

B SMART

Out of the Weeds

As I've discussed, because I'm so detail-oriented and I sweat the small stuff, I can get pulled into the weeds, which is not a place I should be. When I am not focused on the big picture because I'm stuck on small details, I also feel the wolves at the end of the bed: the feeling that something is going to go wrong because I'm looking the other way, distracted by something that is taking my eye off the ball. Does this happen to you? I have a tendency to do too many things myself, which is not the best use of my time. Because of my speed and efficiency, I can get things done faster than anyone I know. That makes it's hard for me to ask someone else to do something like write an email or pick up something at the store. I'm also not too big for any job—nothing is beneath me. I will clean a toilet, pick up dog poop, grocery shop, go to the post office, or anything else if it needs doing. The problem is, I allow myself to get sucked into things that take me away from the most important aspects of my business and life. Look at how you are spending your time, and evaluate what is a time suck and what isn't in terms of your success and your well-being. Don't get sucked into things you should not be doing. I always come from a place of yes, but that often requires saying no! The actor Matthew McConaughey told me that sometimes a red light is a green light. I like that. In other words, sometimes you have to say no to one thing so you can say yes to something more important to your business or life. If there is a task you can delegate, then do it! If someone is asking you to do something you simply aren't able to do, say so and say no. We can all minimize tasks in our life that take us away from our goals. Edit out what is not serving you, and ask others for help.

When You Paint a Picture, Make It Accurate

When you feel the wolves getting restless, it's a sign to evaluate what messages you're putting out to the world. It's a time to pull back, keep to yourself, keep yourself honest, and keep yourself humble.

Resist the temptation to reinforce the idea that everything in your life is perfect and pristine, enviable and easy. It's easy to get into that habit, especially if you have any kind of social media profile. This is why I say social media is the devil in a certain way. It enables and even encourages us to create a visual fantasy world of what life is supposed to be like but never is: perfect house, amazing wardrobe, cherubic children, handsome partner, incredible relationships, financial stability, and glowing health. Likewise, spending too much time looking at other people's seemingly perfect online lives is also dangerous because it makes you feel bad about yourself. But none of it is real.

While I don't advocate posting every personal problem on social media or being the wellspring of "poor me" complaints, because that also paints an unrealistic picture, and a negative one, I do think that technology makes it too easy to make things look all good all the time. Way back when, the BlackBerry made it possible for me to create a business on my phone, but it also made it impossible for me to be without my phone—technology is definitely a double-edged sword. We can also become addicted to the feedback we get from our posts, but that approval is transitory and, ultimately, lacks authentic meaning. We're looking for love in all the wrong places. It's fool's gold.

This is one of the reasons I go out of my way to show my fans and followers the many moods of Bethenny on social media. Yes, I have my rare glam moments, when my hair and makeup are extra special and I'm wearing a pretty dress. That *is* real life, because I do have to get decked out on occasion. And, as I've said, I don't wear makeup *ever* or do anything to my hair unless I'm getting paid. That means those glam moments are part of business. That's why I am deliberate about posting the times when I'm in bed, my hair pulled back, glasses on, makeup off, relaxed in my favorite well-worn sweats. People want to be told the truth, especially about people they have invested in, whether that's in the form of time or money. If people see you're being honest about that, they feel more secure that you're being honest when you tell them about a new product or idea. They also feel better about themselves and their flaws and shortcomings, because you haven't created a false picture of your life that demands perfection. The more you filter yourself, the more quickly they will be willing to pull you down when they realize what you have been showing them isn't the truth.

I became somewhat well known when I first appeared on a season of the *Housewives*. My prior involvement in *The Apprentice: Martha Stewart* didn't make me into a well-known person, but the *Housewives* did in a way. Viewers seemed to notice that I was different from the other cast members. In media commentary about the show, fans pointed out that I spoke in a different way from the other cast members; I was less guarded and more straightforward. I understood from that recognition that I had a responsibility to those viewers and any future audience to continue to be real and transparent to the best of my ability. It's a personal conflict, because I know what sells: sex, controversy, perfection. But I just can't do it to my people.

People count on me to be honest and authentic. Effective marketing is personal. Customers buy my products and consume my media because they trust me. When I first started on the *House-wives* and was building a brand and products, I was honest about being broke and alone. People connected to me. Which is why, in turn, they connected to my books and products, and to me as a business person and an entrepreneur. I can't lose

> When you feel the wolves getting restless, it's a sign to evaluate what messages you're putting out to the world.

touch with that. If I do, I will break a bond, an unspoken agreement I have with my fans, customers, and colleagues to always be straight with them.

When people get bullish about themselves and think they're hot stuff, they might start to overexpose themselves with braggadocio. You may have seen this behavior in a friend or loved one. It can be painful to watch. The person might be excited about a promotion at work, or a stock market score, or some other kind of lucky windfall. They brag and show off. They believe their own hype, get high on their own supply. And then something goes wrong: the stock market tanks, the job doesn't work out, their significant other dumps them. The bubble is unexpectedly burst, and it hurts. And people looking at this from the outside feel a certain amount of satisfaction because the picture that was painted seems superficial and fraudulent.

I talked to Jim Cramer, investor and host of *Mad Money* on CNBC, about this subject and how it ties into success. "We all need time off to do great. There are self-made 'thousand-aires' who think the secret to becoming a millionaire is to never take time off. Wrong. When you relax and retreat, that's when you declutter your mind. I am absolutely convinced that when you start to question yourself, you're tired and you need a break to get fired up again." That's exactly what I do when I feel the wolves waiting: I need time away to collect myself and to destress. That's when new ideas come, and the nervousness I feel about the wolves dissipates.

When I look around and see the boxes checked off, the business humming, new products launching, and deals coming together, I can also feel the wolves getting restless. That's when something is going to get fucked up. When you feel high on life, it's time to pull back to be in your relationship, with your family and your child, your friends, and most of all, yourself. These are the times I go inward. I become calm and quiet. That's when I stop and take a break.

We all need to give ourselves that space. For me, it means a long walk on the beach, meditating, relaxing with my daughter and Paul. The Hamptons is my happy place. If I'm with my daughter, Bryn, we stay in our pajamas, make a fire if the weather is cool, watch movies, go for a horseback ride, go sledding or ice skating in winter, or swim in the summer. We cook and laugh together. I play with my dogs, Biggy and Smallz. Dogs are a great antidote for anxiety.

The Media Is an Incredible Tool—and It Has Sharp Claws

The media is a bear. Don't poke it. I went through a horrendous divorce that took nine years. I couldn't get off the ride. I wanted everyone to stop talking about it, but because it was lengthy and complicated, and some of it played out in open court, stories continued to surface. I know that people love reading tabloid-y stories about well-known people. Admittedly, I brought the attention onto myself because I am a public person. I asked to be a public person; I worked hard to become a public person. Having your crappy divorce covered in the media from the *Times* to the tabloids is part of the package. I get it, but that doesn't make it any easier. I have a young daughter, and I didn't want her exposed to these stories and the gossip, and that hurt most of all. I'm a big girl, I can take it. But she is an innocent in all of it.

As a public person, I also use the media and do so strategically, to my advantage. When I want to promote, sell, or launch a product, I go to the media. The media has been and continues to be an important tool in my relief work. When used wisely, it is an incredible beast for its sheer force, power, and influence. The media can elect presidents and destroy them. It tells stories that inspire and delight, inform us and make us angry; it can comfort us during times of crisis. Undeniably, the Kardashians are billionaires because of the media. Undeniably, Justin Bieber became a sensation because of the media. And undeniably, the media, in the form of television, promoted my cocktail and helped land me on the covers of *Forbes* and *Entrepreneur* magazine. Amazing things have happened to me because of the bear.

Relationships and how they are chronicled on social media are especially interesting. Here's how it goes: boy meets girl or girl meets girl or boy meets boy, and one or both of them are so excited about it that they need to tell the world. Just look at Instagram and see all the images and captions that advertise the greatest loves in history—at least it seems so. You're in such love you need to post every thumb-sucking moment of the relationship, ink tatting, present bought, and flower given. The posts become about showing everybody else how great your life is, which is the entire basis of social media. As in, I'm so happy, I'm so lucky, we're having so much sex. It's so romantic. He/she loves me so much. Look how great my life is! It's the filtering of the faces, the showing of the money and all of the stuff you have. And you get so much reinforcement and approval from it, it's intoxicating.

It can also make other people feel bad about themselves. When something cracks in your life or relationship—you break up, lose your looks, don't get the part in the movie, get fired, your kid gets arrested, *you* get arrested—all that gloating you did is painful to look back on. If you're a normal person and not an egocentric braggart, you feel wounded, hurt, ashamed, and embarrassed. Life lesson: If you're not going to flaunt the bad, don't flaunt the good.

I have had public relationships in my life. I understand that the people who follow me are interested in my personal life. I know that some of them, perhaps many of them, believe I live a fairy-tale life. I had a show called *Bethenny Ever After*, which ran between 2010 and 2012 on Bravo, that chronicled my marriage to my ex-husband and the birth of my daughter. At the time, it was the highest rated premiere in Bravo's history. When things were good, they were good. Everybody was on board, viewers thought I'd found my fairy-tale life, and they were rooting for me. Many of them knew I had had a difficult childhood, that I had worked hard to get out of debt and win financial freedom. I had done it with my own grit and determination. I didn't want to do the show, and it wasn't a happy ending. It was hard not only to go through a complicated and acrimonious divorce, but to talk to my fans about the breakup of that marriage and the struggles, which they could see play out in the public square. It was devastating to go through that time both legally and emotionally, but I never had any pretense on that show or afterward that I was perfect, or that my life was perfect, or that I was better than my fans. And that's why my people, my fans, stood by me.

People connect to you, and they want to know the details. In my case, people have invested time in listening to me talk about my margarita or my other products, they've sat in front of the television to watch my show, they've supported me. They feel they deserve to know what's going on in my love life, my personal

> Be honest and authentic. Stay true to your values.

life. I understand that. I share what I can, but I don't share everything. Because I'm honest, most respect it.

The problem with other well-known people, both on a large and small scale, whether it's the neighbor in your cul-de-sac or Brad and Angelina, is that they share all the great stuff but hide the bad stuff. Maintaining an image becomes more important than reality, and that's one of the reasons people have nervous breakdowns. They prioritize looking like they have a great life over actually creating a great life. It takes a personal emotion toll, and it does a disservice to their relationships, whether it's with family and friends or fans and followers. However, there are some people who are thirsty for attention and approval, and cannot live without it.

One day, when everyone is blindsided because the person has gotten divorced or gone into rehab, or lost their job or got canceled or has another problem that seems to come out of nowhere, the wall comes down and people feel disappointed, as if they've been had. Because they have been. Of course, all of this is no one's business but the people going through it. Celebrities, like everyone else, don't have to tell us everything. At issue is how much we invest in a narrative that is presented as authentic. The media shows us the pictures of the roses and the relationship, the wedding and the honeymoon. When it doesn't work out, the media wants to know everything, wants to spill all the tea and show all the problems that were hidden. An unsettling cycle of fantasy and truth begins—and also, frankly, a lack of trust in the people whom you thought you knew.

Many public people—whether it's the president of the local PTA or a national figure—are scared about revealing the truth. I understand that. We all want to protect ourselves, but we set ourselves up for some vicious bites if the story we tell is so carefully controlled and curated that it just looks like a complete sham when one crack turns into a crater. That's why you have to be careful about how your private self and your public self operate in the world.

When I became engaged to Paul, I didn't announce it to the media. For me, having been through a public engagement and marriage, I knew that the news would be about the ring and what I was wearing: all of the romance and window dressing and none of the seriousness around our commitment. The external accoutrements are the wrong things to emphasize when you get engaged. I believe that the wedding business is bad for the marriage business, because the wedding business puts the focus on all the wrong things in a relationship, and not the right thing, which is a solemn union between two people. It puts a lot of expectations about relationships under a false or ephemeral light. Because Paul and I made the decision not to invite people into our relationship, we've been able to maintain a certain level of privacy around it.

I also understand that people want to know about the details: What does the ring look like, how big is it, how did he propose, where were you, what were you wearing, where will you be married, what will your dress look like? People want to be part of the process. The other side is that the sharing of the moment and the glamorous details can make people feel bad about themselves, as in why her and not me? I am there for it: I have been alone and lonely at many stages of my life.

The media wants well-known people to share their personal lives because "intimacy" sells. And it helps those people too, no doubt about it. When things are going well, it helps sell the latest movie, elevate the brand, win a local election, bring in customers. This is a feature of the media and also a flaw. When something goes wrong, the same media trashes the relationship to bits, and the movie and the products and the brand can go into the bin with it.

The media is a great seducer. It's like being invited into this enticing den where all the glittering details are laid out on display, and then it switches to darkness, and the fairy tale is over. I find this cycle unsettling, a little bit scary. I have chosen overall in my life to try to be as private as possible while being a public person. One of the misconceptions about me is that I am not private because I've been on reality TV, I have a podcast, and I do use social media. But I'm not interested in being famous or photographed.

I am intensely private, fiercely private. It's why I have such a small staff; it's why I have such a small infrastructure. I do not trust many people. That trait can be a double-edged sword when it comes to the media. But we're all addicted to the ride to some degree. When you think about your public persona, consider what you want it to accomplish. This holds true for everyone. If you're in any kind of business, you want everything you do publicly to reflect truthfully on you and your brand. You want your integrity to shine through. Be honest and authentic. Stay true to your values. Think about the people looking at your media and consider their needs. Share something useful. Have humility.

12

It's Worth the Risk to Build It Because They Will Come

I AM A TRUE BELIEVER THAT IF YOU BUILD IT THEY WILL COME, BUT you *do* have to build it. And creating new things involves risk. Risk-taking is a part of business and life. It can be scary or exhilarating or both, but one thing is clear: to learn new things, achieve something great, create and innovate, or build bigger and better, there is always risk involved. Even when you're planning on doing something you've done before, there is an element of the unknown. I've been snowboarding for twenty-plus years, but every time I do it, I'm taking a chance that I might fall or be injured. Every time I do yoga, it feels like the first time. Likewise, there are no guarantees that your ideas or efforts will pan out, and when you do something that looks like it's outside of your wheelhouse, there is even greater pressure on you. Doesn't matter. You have to be strategic about risks, but you have to follow your heart and your passions too. Like I say—sometimes you have to jump to fly.

All meaningful endeavors I've undertaken have taken me off of a conventional, safe path: starting a baking business; going on the *Housewives* not once but twice and walking away from it; creating a ready-to-drink margarita cocktail and marketing it and then selling it; developing a new television show; buying, renovating, and selling houses; doing stand-up comedy! There is little I've done that has kept me on a conventional, safe path. On my podcast, I say what I mean, and sometimes I get in trouble for it and have to clarify later, but the upside of that creative outlet is so great, I'm comfortable with the risks of being outspoken. Listeners are appreciative of my candor because what I say resonates with them. Despite occasional media reports on some of my more "controversial" comments, I haven't been "canceled." My listeners keep tuning in—the public is the only entity that can cancel you if you have created independence and are self-supporting. So far, so good.

Transitioning from being known as a "reality TV star" to a business person was a risk because I knew that it would require an effort to be taken seriously. In the beginning of that journey, I wasn't, and the wolves in the media and social media were sometimes vocal about their skepticism. Honestly, I *shouldn't* have been taken seriously in the beginning; I had no value. Or I didn't know the value I would have yet. Bravo offered me a contract for $7,250 for the entire first season of the *Housewives*—which was a lot for me. It was a fair price because I knew that I wanted to be an independent business person and an entrepreneur, and I wanted the freedom from being shackled that comes with that. I wanted to keep my interest in everything I created, and to have the ability to expand in any direction I saw fit. I was clear about those goals, so the risk of doing the *Housewives,* the exposure of my personal life that it involved, the amount of time it would demand, and the small amount of money I would be paid were all worth it to me because it was a chance to gain exposure for my burgeoning career.

When I decided to do the show, there weren't other people who had already done reality shows. It was rare for someone to appear on multiple reality shows at that time. I exploited the opportunity in the best ways I could—I talked about Skinnygirl, I advertised it as much as possible. I used my time on television to build what was important to me, which was not fame or celebrity, but the chance to promote myself as a natural foods chef. The risk paid off. Before the show, the only offer I had received was from Pepperidge Farm to be a natural chef spokesperson. The offer was close to $100,000, which seemed like millions to me because I was broke. So it was a risk to do the *Housewives*, which showed women drinking and arguing, and Pepperidge Farm is a mainstream, family-oriented brand. That partnership worked out.

> Everything meaningful that I've done has been a risk.

So let's talk about risk—why you should take it, how to be smart about it, and what it can do for your business aspirations and goals, and, frankly, for your personal evolution and growth.

Did You Hear the One About Doing Stand-up Comedy?

I have long loved stand-up comedy. I love to laugh, and people tell me I'm funny. I'm pretty fearless too—even though I am a loner and often an introvert, I'm not always socially awkward (although I can be). I'm good at connecting with people when I want to express something, and I'm unafraid to approach people or make myself known. My personal interest in comedy led me to take comedy sketch classes at the famous Groundlings Theater & School in Los Angeles, and improv classes at Second City. When I was a student at New York University my dream was to become an intern at *Saturday Night Live*—I still have a dream of hosting the show. I actually was offered an internship at *Saturday Night Live*, but at the time NYU did not give credit for that internship, so *SNL* did not offer it, saying they could only do so if I received college credit for it. It's a regret that I didn't force the matter. If it were today, I would not have given up so easily. I would have talked to the dean and pushed through to make it work.

Comedy is a dream that has stayed with me. During the pandemic, Paul and I were talking about something called a nonfungible token, or NFT, which is a piece of digital information that can be a video or a photograph or some other kind of data. Paul asked me about what I could do as an NFT that no one has seen before. I said to Paul, what about stand-up comedy? After all, I say witty things on television and on my podcast, and I've taken comedy classes. But I've never done an actual comedy routine for public consumption. Paul put together a shoot with a long-standing director of photography-producer whom I knew from the *Housewives,* and he shot a video NFT of me doing stand-up. I still have it, and it's never been seen by anyone except Paul and me. But it gave me a little practice for what would happen next.

We were still in pandemic mode in April 2021 when I had the opportunity to do a short stand-up routine at New York Comedy Club in Manhattan's East Village on the first night it reopened after the initial pandemic shutdown. I had ten days to prepare my material, which would be different from what I did for the NFT. Even though places like New York Comedy Club were starting to open up, and New Yorkers were beginning to emerge from their cocoons and go out again, there was still anxiety about the COVID virus. What I didn't think about is that people in the club would have to sit six feet apart and wear masks, which is not that comical. Stand-up comedy is about people feeding off one another's energy, and if I had thought about the protocols I might not have done it. I thought it was worth the risk given that masks were required and social distancing was in force. Besides, once I said I was going to do it, I was all in. I am not the kind of person who folds on a promise.

Planning was involved, which is important for risk-takers. The set would be seven minutes, in front of an audience of about forty guests. I started getting organized and writing down some ideas. I went with topics I knew that I could land. What I needed was structure and an approach. Next, I called and texted comedy people whom I respected, including Ellen DeGeneres, Kathy Griffin, Chris Rock, Whitney Cummings, and Kevin Nealon, asking each for three pieces of wisdom. Everyone responded immediately, which gave me so much respect for the art form and the passion that comedians have for it. Wow!

Chris Rock told me to know what I was starting with and what I was ending with. The rest is a flow. He advised me not to bring a lot of people. Kathy Griffin told me, *do* bring in people who set you up for feeling funny. Ellen told me to keep my material relatable and accessible. One comedian told me to take the mike off the stand and put the stand behind me. Another told me they liked the stand because it can be used as a prop. I liked the conflicting advice I received. It helped me prepare and feel good about the material I'd come up with. I used the advice to create my own tool box for comedy. This is similar to what I offer on my podcast. People hear a variety of advice and viewpoints, and they can take from it and put together what's relevant to them and make their own plan.

I took all the ingredients, and the advice I received, and used them to create my own recipe. Comedy, like life and business, is about being prepared and having an understanding of what you're doing before jumping in. I could not predict the reaction, but I felt prepared to take the risk. I had practiced the routine in front of Paul, in front of my dogs and a group of stuffed animals, in the mirror. I was prepared, but nervous going in. Like many learning experiences in life, the idea of doing it was worse than actually doing it—something important to remember when you're about to take a risk. Jump to fly!

I told stories that highlighted the absurdities and ironies of everyday contemporary life. I talked about when you go to a coffee shop to get your latte, the counter is plastic, the chairs are covered in plastic, the cup the drink goes in is plastic, the card you pay with—plastic. But the straw you get is paper. That's where they draw the line. By the time you're halfway through your beverage, it's like drinking out of a paper airplane.

People were laughing, and I felt good. I continued.

I talked about how I wanted to meet kale's publicist. Great job. Everywhere you're assaulted by kale. Kale massages, kale Caesar salad, kale cocktails, baby kale because the big kale had children, kale-dashians. Kale every which way but Sunday.

It was such fun, such a high. I don't know whether I will do it again, but I know I *can* do it. Having the fearlessness and courage to do that set taught me so much about myself.

Those seven minutes on stage built my confidence. I proved to myself that I am never too old to learn or do something new and outside of my routine experience. It also fulfilled a dream of mine, which cannot be underestimated. Don't go through life without checking off some of those boxes.

I took all the ingredients, and the advice I received, and used them to create my own recipe.

Every person I spoke to about doing this told me they had the dream of doing it too. It's not as easy as it sounds; otherwise all the people who want to do it would. It also made it easier for me to take other risks in the future. Risk-taking, like doing a stand-up comedy routine, builds your risk muscles. I also have a renewed admiration and respect for the craft of comedy and those who do it.

B SMART

Prepare, Prepare, Prepare!

Set yourself up for success when taking risks. With stand-up comedy, I applied myself. I researched and prepared my material, asked for advice, created my routine, timed it, and practiced until I felt comfortable to go on stage. It wasn't that I needed people to help me with how to be funny, but to set myself up for success by being prepared in the right way. If I am prepared I don't worry about the result. I feel good about whatever I am doing if I feel prepared and ready. Here are some ways to get ready to jump, fly, and soar:

1. *Test the waters.* Before I did my actual live stand-up routine, I practiced, as I said. But I'd also been laying the groundwork for a while—by taking classes, watching a lot of comics, and practicing.

2. *Think about the worst-case scenario.* Thinking about potential outcomes actually alleviates fear. Once you go through in your mind all of the potential pitfalls, you can prepare for them (see above), or you demystify or disarm their power. What's the worst that could happen to me if no one laughed at my jokes? No one would laugh at my jokes. That's it. My life wouldn't change. No big deal. I could cope with that.

3. *Create a plan B (C, D, and E).* As you consider what could go wrong, use those pain points to create a backup plan. How you respond to potential outcomes can help you devise other ways to take the risk. Creating alternative ways to take a risk with a new business idea, for instance, can lead to new ways of looking at things. Using stand-up as an example, maybe I could have done a routine with someone else as a team, to take some of the pressure off. There is more than one way to peel a banana.

4. *Own mistakes and learn from them.* Failures are teaching tools if you look at them that way. What can you do better next time? How can you tweak what you did? I think I did pretty well in my stand-up routine, but if I ever do it again I will think about everything from what I wore to my pacing and timing between punch lines. There is always room for improvement!

Deciding What Risk Is Worth Taking

Successful risk is knowing what is worth risking and where you can make mistakes, and where you can't. I talked to two powerful women about smart risk on my podcast: Sheryl Sandberg, the Facebook COO, and powerhouse technology journalist Kara Swisher. Both shared valuable insights. Sheryl talked about companies as they grow bigger, but her insights are applicable to whatever stage you're in. "As companies get bigger, you need to separate out the places you can take risk from the places you can't," she said. She told a story about having dinner with the CEO of a major airline. After coming off of three flights that had been delayed for a catering problem and luggage processing, she was frustrated. She asked him why big airlines get what seemed like no-brainers to her, food and luggage, so wrong. What he told her was surprising, but made an impact.

"In a huge part of my business, there is no room for error. None. Zero. Zip. Those planes have to take off, we cannot take off with a mechanical problem, we cannot have a maintenance problem, there is no room for error. All of our errors per catering and luggage, all of the delays caused by luggage are not life-threatening. That's where we can absorb some risk," he told her. Sheryl continued, "I went back to Facebook and I said, okay, we have got to figure out what's plane maintenance and what's catering and luggage. We made a privacy claim that ensures when you post something just to your best friends, it doesn't get shared to the world, it just gets posted to your best friends," she told them. That's plane maintenance, making sure that the technology fulfills that promise to users.

"When we roll out a new shopping product, and it doesn't have all the features, we can roll with it. That's catering and luggage." In other words, the shopping function is a feature, not maintenance. It's not life-threatening if you don't have every bell and whistle when you roll it out. So there's where you can take your risks. "Catering and luggage doesn't have to be perfect, we can put out products, and iterate and learn." In other words, you don't have to build a 747 every time, but you do have to know the difference between a 747 and a rolling cart when you're deciding where to take risks.

Kara Swisher talked about taking a risk early in her journalism career that set her on a path to being called "the most powerful tech journalist" in the world. She's been a risk-taker since she was a little girl in the third grade, when she walked out of the classroom one day because she knew what was being taught "and wouldn't come back until they came up with something fresh."

When she entered journalism, it was in DC as a reporter at the *Washington City Paper*, and then as an intern at the powerful

Washington Post. "I was headed for a traditional career covering politics, because that's what the winners did at the time. It was the big game at the *Post*." The problem is, Kara wasn't interested in politics. "There's so much closeness and bullshit, I couldn't imagine typing that every day," she told me. It was of course a risk to turn away from a respected career path, one that might have brought her to powerful places in the world of journalism and reporting. Instead, she took a different and less certain path.

"When I saw the internet for the first time, it was very *Star Trek*, and I was a fan of *Star Trek* and *Star Wars*. It was going to be big." Not everyone saw what Kara saw. "Someone said it was going to be like CB radio and I said no. There will be a worldwide information system in your pocket. Everyone ignored me. I saw it before other people. I was certainly one of the people in media who said it." What do you do when you see things other people don't see? You take the risk and go after it, and that's what Kara did. "I am entrepreneurial. I thought, where can I go to write about this? I have to get to Silicon Valley." That's when she went to the *Wall Street Journal*, moved to San Francisco, and began to cover the businesses and people who were part of the "start-up" that became what we know today as the worldwide web, the internet, ecommerce, and social media.

Her advice: "Be your genuine self. Don't edit yourself. Women especially do this because we're raised to be people-pleasers. Don't let your talents go to waste. It's so freeing to be in charge of your destiny on some level, to rise and fall on your abilities. Tune out your self-doubts and understand that it's okay to fail. It's like that Thomas Edison quote, 'I have not failed. I've just found ten thousand ways that won't work.'"

Here, here.

Risk Means Sometimes Saying You're Sorry

Cultivating a fan base takes legwork. I used to spend a great deal of time on the road, doing meet-and-greets, book signings, and bottle signings. My fans are sensible and aspirational. They make an effort to look nice. They know everything they can about me, and they appreciate my honesty. When I meet a fan, they always ask questions like, "How's your daughter?" or "How are Biggy and Smallz?" (My beloved dogs!) That means a lot to me. I appreciate that they care about me, and in return I care about them. Reality television brings me into people's lives, so of course those who invest in watching me on television feel a connection to me. They are curious about my life and my well-being. I appreciate that fact.

But. I am an aggressive person. I am unfiltered. Sometimes things come out of my mouth that can offend people. You can't always play it safe, but you can't be reckless.

When you take communication risks, which I take all the time, the results can and will affect your fans, and people in general. It can have an impact in the way they think about and respond to you and your brand. I have a voice, and I sometimes don't realize how powerful it is. All of us can make ripples or waves when we decide to express an opinion or say or do something that can be perceived as controversial. My advice it to make sure it is worth saying. Sometimes when you go out on a limb and do or say something that your fans (or friends, or neighbors) disapprove of, they want you to apologize. They may also want to control the *way* in which you apologize. People in general don't like an apology such as, "I'm sorry if I hurt you." That's not what they're looking for. They want you to be more sincere in your acknowledgment that you said or did something hurtful. I understand that because it happened on the *Housewives*.

In March 2021, I took a risk and voiced my opinion about Meghan Markle's primetime interview with Oprah Winfrey. I was skeptical about her journey as a departing member of the royal family. I voiced this skepticism on my Twitter account, where it reached my 1.5 million followers, and many other people as well, since my comments were picked up by the media. A major A-list celebrity reached out to me and told me that I needed to apologize to Meghan or retract what I had said. Two others texted me to say that I was spot on. It was flattering to me that this A-list person thought to make the call, because it meant that I had a voice, and that people listen when I speak. That's why I have to be careful about the things I say and try my best to measure my words. But I am outspoken— so the struggle is real! Many other people, both well-known and civilians, told me privately that they agreed with my assessment. But the timing of my comment was off, and the way I voiced my opinion could have been better. Sometimes we don't always realize or think about who could be listening, and we have to be conscious and considerate of their feelings. I am tough but fair. I do not want to be cruel to anyone, even while I am being outspoken.

Experiences like the Meghan Markle episode teach me something about my fans and my own communication. I want to think about their point of view and apply it to future communications. Always think carefully about how what you say and do will affect others. As I tell my daughter, actions have consequences.

I also reach out to people individually and say I understand I hurt you and I'm sorry that I upset you. I understand where you're coming from. This kind of acknowledgment and apology goes a long way because it addresses what people want when you do something that bothers them: they want to be heard.

You gain or connect with associates, customers, and fans one person at a time. Reaching out to Jane from Des Moines or Julie from Detroit is more important and more authentic than issuing a statement apology to the press, which is meaningless and disingenuous. The point is, it's the connection, the sincerity of what you're saying, and the promise to do better in the future that are important, and not the apology itself. Connecting with people can put things into perspective.

> All of us can make ripples or waves when we decide to express an opinion or say or do something that can be perceived as controversial.

Know Your Value — and Expect to Get It

In business and in life you must make sure that people don't take advantage of your good nature, generosity, and enthusiasm. That requires taking a stand, which can be risky. But allowing someone to take advantage of you is on you. Understand what you are worth and expect to get it. A reputation for being someone who can't be taken advantage of in any transaction or negotiation, business or personal, makes you stronger and commands respect. It is a journey that never ends—there will always be someone who will try to take advantage of you; it's human nature. Spot it and stop it. Yes, it is a risk, because when you ask for what you want or deserve, you might get a no. It's still worth it.

I'll give you one example that definitely has to do with being well known, but my strategy applies to making sure you are paid what you are worth for a job. You should get a fair return for the time and expertise you invest.

Not that long ago, a new company named Cameo reached out to me to ask if I wanted to be a part of the start-up. The American video-sharing website is headquartered in Chicago and was founded in 2016 by three people. The site enables fans to hire celebrities from various arenas, including sports, business, reality television, and film, to send personalized video messages to their friends and family. By mid-2020, more than 30,000 well-known people had joined the platform.

I was a bit concerned about its potential, but on the other hand, it can be hard to know where a new social media idea will go. There is always a chance that a new platform will be a breakout success, and a site like Cameo could become valuable. I thought about the idea of becoming involved for a few days, and came to the conclusion that I would do it but only if I received some equity in the company. For me, it made more sense to have a part of a company that might explode rather than just be paid as a work-for-hire person, which is the way Cameo works. The company charges users a set fee for personal or business messages, and that price varies from person to person (based on how popular they are). My involvement wasn't that interesting unless I had a stake in the company.

Despite many attempts to talk to them about my interest, Cameo wasn't paying attention, or at least the people I was talking to didn't address my actual interest—investing in the idea itself. Paul even talked to Cameo on my behalf about acquiring an interest in the company—that's his wheelhouse. Finally, we were told that the company was nearly fully subscribed for the first round of venture capital funding. The partners in the company explained to us that they could allow ten people who were part of Cameo to invest a certain amount of money in it during the next round of funding. Cameo definitely wanted me involved; I was a "get"—a person whom they knew would attract paying users. It also wanted me to pursue others to join, and I actually brought them Katie

Couric and Michael Rapaport, one of the top ten social media earners, and a few other high-profile people.

Eventually, we were able to pay for some equity in the company.

Parallel to this was a great deal of press generated by Cameo about my involvement with the company, the details of which had not yet been finalized. I felt like I was being used as part of a sales pitch in the many articles about the website that appeared in both the business and general press, and it bothered me because I wasn't being compensated to promote this business. I had paid to invest in it. It wasn't fair and it didn't feel right. I had paid to get equity in the company, but that didn't mean they could use me in press. I told Cameo that unless I received more equity in the company, they needed to stop using my name and involvement to win more business. I felt that I should get some monetary reward for bringing them business, and for the use of my name in publicity. After all, I had paid for a stake in the company, I did not pay to become one of its spokespeople.

Bottom line, Cameo would either have to give me more equity or pay me in order to continue to use my name in the press and promotion.

Yet Cameo continued to ignore this request while pushing me to do things on their behalf. "You don't understand," I told them. "I paid for my equity. That does not give you the right to continue to use my name or me in your publicity."

Cameo held another round of funding, Series B Funding, and we were able to be in for that round. Then, the company bloated in the pandemic. It gained value that was twenty times what Paul and I had invested in it. I called Mark Cuban and another knowledge-able friend and asked them how much of our equity we should sell, and each offered a thoughtful number. We took the average of all the answers and sold part of our equity, making twenty times our money, which is a big return. We later sold the rest, and are now out of that business.

I take the same approach when other companies want me to get involved. I make it clear that I am not interested in being a work-for-hire person. I want to own a part of something that looks promising. Yes, it is a risk, but one I am willing to take. I do my homework, and am strategic about what I am willing to lose if the investment doesn't work out. Had I known how much financial *and* brand equity I could have created by getting a piece of the *Housewives*...it boggles my mind. If I had only known the value of the Bravo network, I would have insisted on getting equity in that entity as well. There is no guarantee that I would have gotten a piece of those businesses, but at least I would have tried when I was asked to come back. I would have also made sure that I was not used to make money for a business that wasn't compensating me for that use properly. Overall, the Cameo experience was a positive one.

Too many people allow themselves to be taken advantage of in this way, and we all need to become part of the Not Fucking Around Crew. You don't have to be well known to benefit from the insight of this story, which is to know your value and expect it to be met. If you see someone benefiting from you, your work, your skills and talents, maybe you should think about what that means. Is there something else that you can and should be asking for? If you have taken on new responsibilities at your job, and you are getting positive results, it may be time to talk to your boss about a raise. If you are helping to create a new business, make sure your share of any profits is in line with the effort you're contributing. You need a tenacious spirit as you go through life. It's not enough to see the big picture, you have to *act* on it too. You have to make it clear that you're not here to play games. You're in it for real, and you're paying attention.

Find the Balance

Risk is also about finding the right personal balance. Taking risks and measuring your success is part of learning who you are, where your boundaries lie, and living life in a way that respects the truth of who you are. I want to be free and unshackled. I've always been this way. All the work I do has this goal in mind. Over the summer of 2021, I was on a short vacation and ran into a well-known couple. I noted they had a party of people with cameras and other equipment around them. At first I thought the paparazzi were following them around. What I discovered as we talked was that this crew of people were their own personal paparazzi, which included photographers, stylists, and makeup people. These people would control the shots and feed them to the media or post the pictures on the women's social media accounts.

Later, I found out from a successful branding person that there is not a celebrity in Hollywood who does not travel around with their own photographers and stylists to be there for them at every level, or they call the media to photograph them. I have not done that, and I never will. I don't want to be shackled in that or any other way. I don't want or need an entourage. I'm hitting my stride, and I want to make my own decisions. It's not who I am anymore. I'm a less-is-more person. Maybe it hurts me not to have this level of activity around me. I don't think it does, however, and even then it wouldn't be worth it to me.

I know what I want: financial freedom and contentment, and the power to have an impact on others. I want a strong business and a robust philanthropic effort that continually works to meet the needs of victims and first responders. I will take the risks necessary to achieve those goals, to expand my knowledge, and to test my limits. I want to inspire you to have that too by doing the following.

- Taking risks but always preparing for them.
- Accepting responsibility for the results of your actions, whether good or bad.
- Being accountable to yourself and others who are affected by your decisions.
- Not giving up—failure may not be an option, but it's a reality.

13

Fewer Buckets Full

I AM A DOER. WHEN I'M WORKING, I AM *WORKING*. IT'S A NON-stop hustle. Time is money, and I try to spend both wisely. I take things one step at a time. It's how I wrote this book—one chapter at a time. When I clean out my drawers and organize them, it's one by one. I explain to everyone, let's not worry about the big picture right now, let's get going first. You have to get on the road and get started. I'm project-based so if I can't sleep at night, I do a deep dive into researching whatever I'm thinking about at the time. If I am working with an interior designer on a house project, I can find twenty couch options overnight and send the links to her the next morning. I'll find the perfect bathing suit for Bryn with a few clicks on my phone. I do things in pieces or sections. Hunt and gather. Small bites. If I'm working on a book, I edit chapter by chapter. I even chew my food slowly and thoroughly. After my daughter was born, if she took a nap, I took a nap too. Even five minutes between meetings can be productive. Since I flip houses too, while I was writing this book I had appointments to look at five investment properties. I took my book notes with me so I could work on them between appointments in the car (don't worry, I wasn't driving and reading at the same time).

I can stop moving physically, but my mind never stops, and this can be challenging for me. I love to be alone as a way of clearing my head. I do yoga, meditate, or take a walk on the beach, but I am always thinking. This predisposition to always have things running through my mind is likely related to my perfectionism and quest for order. Internally, I'm always working through something, solving a problem, or generating ideas. I might be looking for a reasonably priced, good size industrial steam cleaner because I have dogs that sometimes pee in the house. I find one and think, maybe I should make a better one. How can I market this product? Say I want to sell a personal margarita blender that makes drinks like the ones you get at a bar. I hunt it down online and order one, and think about how I might be able to do it better. My personal life is constantly blended with my business life. I am solution-based in life and work.

This can lead to something I call too many buckets, half full. Meaning there are too many things going on and none of them are getting the attention they deserve. What I want is fewer buckets full, meaning less is more!

I talked to Ian Schrager, entrepreneur and cofounder of the iconic Studio 54, hotelier, and real estate developer, who is credited with cocreating the "boutique hotel" category of accommodation, about the idea of nonstop thinking—about work, projects, ideas, passions, family, all the things. Like me, Ian says he sweats the small stuff, which is great. But it can lead to lots of half-empty buckets if you're not careful, even though there is good reason to look at the details.

"I pay attention to the little things because you don't know what will be the one thing that viscerally touches someone in your business, so everything is important. Everything [in business] is a matter of life and death," he says. I'm right there with him. There's a big but, however. "I made sacrifices for my success early in my career. I worked all the time, and as a result, I did not have balance."

"Now I'm older, I do have the balance that comes with wisdom. Our physical reactions might be slower but the mental capacity of wisdom increases with age. The secret to life is finding balance." LOL! "You need a good business, but you also need a good family, you need to love the person you're living with, you need hobbies, friends, kids. If you don't have that in your life, you are not truly happy, like I am now," he explains.

The lack of balance also led him and his original business partner, Steve Rubell, to make unwise choices with the nightclub they were running in Manhattan. In June 1979, Ian and Steve were charged with tax evasion, obstruction of justice, and conspiracy for reportedly skimming nearly $2.5 million in unreported income from Studio 54's receipts. In January 1980, both men were sentenced to three and a half years in prison and a $20,000 fine each for the tax evasion charge. Ian served eighteen months. Going to jail is no small affair, but this story reminds me of an important rule: make mistakes when your business is small. That unbridled hubris, if it had been demonstrated later on when Ian's business became much bigger, would likely have meant a much harsher judgment and a longer jail term.

Ian's imprisonment did have a silver lining. "Before jail, I thought the rules did not apply to me and I could do what I needed to do for success. Jail gave me a year-long forced interlude where I could rest and reflect. That is when I decided to go into the hotel business," he said.

In times of aberration there will be seeds planted and trees will flourish. I can't compare jail to the pandemic of 2020 exactly, but there are some similarities. When you are forced to retreat for any reason, it gives you a chance to look at your buckets—how many you have, how full they are. What's important? What can go? "The pandemic was positive for me," Ian says. "I was able to spend more time with my family, reevaluate, and recalibrate what I want to do. It was an invaluable opportunity, a do-over," he says. You just have to make the time to reevaluate, especially if it's not being forced upon you.

There have been so many times when I have had to say to myself, *Bethenny, you need to step back from everything and regroup.* Recharging my batteries makes me a better leader and a more creative innovator. Even so, I've been known to go past my expiration date. I have to remind myself to rest—unless I reach my breaking point first and have no choice but to come to a screeching halt. That's what happened to me while I was writing this book. I had too many half-full buckets—despite the fact that my philosophy is *fewer buckets full.*

My recent crisis moment occurred after multiple events and obligations in my life and business were happening without enough downtime. Everything came to a head at the same time, and it forced me to look at my buckets. My pandemic year had morphed into whatever 2021 was shaping up to be, and it was all starting to go off the rails right around summertime. Many of us felt stressed in this way during and right after the pandemic and lockdown. We had spent so much time trying to salvage our work, homeschool our kids, and at the same time we began to realize what was truly important and what wasn't. Things started to come into perspective for so many of us. This was a time when the snow globe had been shaken and the world was upside down. I knew and I talked about it. The seeds you plant during times like this will grow into trees that flourish.

I became engaged and started to plan a wedding, which I just could not deal with at a certain point because I felt as though it was a lot of what Paul and I were talking about. There were small moments along the way where it was not a joyful process, which is precisely the true meaning of the commitment. So we said, let's not do this right now. We put the wedding plans on the back burner temporarily.

> There are going to be times when you have to step back from everything and regroup.

Meanwhile, I was not only preparing to write this book, but I had moved to a new state and was in the midst of four property renovations. I was doing a long-distance renovation, fixing up a house for Paul and me to live in. I was also working on a house that I thought I was going to live in but it turned out not to be quite right, and I sold it, which I described earlier. There was yet another property I was renovating for the two of us, but it wasn't quite right either. These misestimations were a result of my not realizing how much I liked Connecticut and how much time I would want to spend there whenever possible. We ended up selling both properties, as I mentioned earlier. That meant I would be moving *again* and renovating yet another house.

What I call my intense perfectionism comes into play when I renovate a house, or do anything, for that matter. The details have to be just right, or I'm not satisfied. As I said, I don't have a junk drawer in my kitchen. There is a place for everything in my house. It's not just that, I want the floors, the cabinetry, the paint on the walls all to be perfect. If I spend any effort on something, I spend all the effort I can. The same perfectionism that never lets me miss anything means that sometimes I can't move forward. My house is immaculate. Every drawer is labeled and organized. I can't move into a place unless it's impeccable to a level that is hard for most people to imagine. The professional organizing companies I've worked with have told me that they have never met anyone more organized than me. This is both an asset and a challenge, because life isn't perfect, but I want my environment to be as close to flawless as possible. I moved a lot as a kid, and it made for a chaotic home and childhood. Having order today is a necessity for me to feel in control and at peace.

At the same time, I had been involved in an unpleasant custody battle involving my young daughter, who is my *world*. She didn't want to separate from me during the pandemic, which was difficult for everyone. The B Strong Initiative relief efforts were in full swing, responding to natural disasters, providing assistance to small businesses affected by the pandemic and shutdowns, and continuing to provide PPE to first responders. I had launched additional Bethenny and Skinnygirl categories. I was executing a reality show in a multi-million-dollar deal with MGM.

My podcast, the result of a massive deal with iHeart, which I discussed earlier, was a hit. I absolutely love doing it. It's one of my favorite things. We had numerous high-profile guests booked when my emotional limit was pressed into overdrive. It wasn't as if I could cancel these guests so I could lie down on an infrared mattress. But something had to give.

There was a lot on my mind the day of my actual breakdown. My staff, who was with me in my house, was pressuring me to do social media posts related to product launches. That involved getting dressed, and having hair and makeup done, and smiling. Lots of smiling. I was also thinking about a commitment to shoot Home Shopping Network episodes for the launch of Skinnygirl frozen pizzas over the coming weekend. I was also planning on going to Nantucket to see Paul's parents and friends as a newly engaged person. That meant we had to schlep an entire suitcase of lighting and sound equipment, along with frozen pizzas, to his house so I could shoot the HSN commercials. I shouldn't have done it this way. It was too jammed up. I should have set limits. I was trying to please everybody, which means you end up pleasing nobody, most importantly, yourself.

I had to set up a pop-up studio and sell pizzas in Paul's kitchen. Once that was done, with the sweat pouring down my arms, I had to get myself together and meet his family and hang out with them as if I'd been relaxing all day in preparation to socialize all evening. While everyone else was having fun in Nantucket, I was shooting a pizza commercial. After the party, I had to pack up all the equipment before I schlepped it all back home.

Let's see…what else was I dealing with? The launch of my cherry juice and coffee syrups and my wine, pizza, and supplements. These were some of the seeds I had planted. And of course, I had to continue selling salad dressing and popcorn and apparel and jeans, not to mention my most important professional job, running the B Strong Initiative, my philanthropy. My initial swimwear launch was a disaster, as I discussed, and had to be reworked so it was something I could actually stand behind and endorse.

I wanted to please everybody.

Do you feel exhausted yet? Out of gas? I was. I hit the wall going 150 miles an hour, and *ka-boom*.

If we're not careful, we can overwhelm ourselves and crack. It usually happens when everyone is pulling at us like crows picking at a carcass in the road. On this one particular afternoon in July 2021, I was the carcass. Everyone around me kept at it until there was no more meat left on the bone. I had to put a stop to it. I had to shut everything down. When you are an authentic person who doesn't hide anything, everybody knows what's going on. After repeating myself a few times, and reinforcing the message that I'd had enough and that I meant it, suddenly the room went quiet. I had told everyone to use the pandemic wisely, and I had done so too. Maybe a little too wisely? I was overwhelmed. The floodgates opened.

Breathe, Bethenny.

To feel that tightness in my body, the dizziness and accompanying anxiety rising up inside me was scary, to be honest. It was like watching a movie, except I was starring in it and I was in peril. At that moment, in the middle of my dining room, surrounding by bed linens, wondering if we had enough for the cottage and the Hamptons, it happened. I had a panic attack. I didn't care about anything anymore. At least I felt that way, in that moment, a first in my career. This is something I'd never experienced before, even when I was driving around in my beat-up $500 car with a broken windshield wondering where I was going to get enough money to pay my rent, bouncing check after check. Even then I felt like I was on top of things. Not this day.

It was a while in coming, and I saw the signs: my digestion was affected, my sleep was poor, my mood was terrible. Everything in me, body and soul, was getting touched by emotional, intellectual, and physical overload. If I kept getting pushed, the machine that is me was going to shut down. I said to everybody standing there, "I'm the golden goose and there will be no more eggs if I break or if I die."

That's when I stopped and retreated. It was just for a few days, but it made all the difference to my emotional health and my ability to get back to business at 100 percent. I rested and recouped.

It was a powerful hit. While it was painful on many levels, I'm glad it happened, because it forced me to think about what was important to me. It reminded me of a life and business principle I had obviously let slip through my fingers: fewer buckets full. It's more effective, *saner*, to have fewer buckets full than multiple buckets half or a quarter full. I could see that so clearly standing in my dining room, fretting about bedsheets. *What was I doing? How did I get to this place?*

When you get off course, as I did, you know things aren't being handled correctly. You have to intervene and go with your gut even though everyone around you is telling you things are great, because everyone's scared to mention what is clearly in front of them. The people that I do business with see the half-filled buckets too, but they look at it as *Bethenny's a workaholic and this is just how she is,* but it's not how I am. It takes courage to say, we interrupt this program to let you know that you're driving without any brakes. That's how it feels, when you have too many half-full buckets everywhere. You don't feel safe, you know something's wrong, and you need to get control. When you have a few carefully chosen buckets, you can keep them filled.

These moments happen to all of us. When they do, we have to realize that things won't get better and we won't recover from exhaustion if we don't stop the presses, stop the madness. After that, we have to set an example not just for others but for ourselves. That means staying off our phones and practicing self-care. That's what I had to do in the middle of that swirl of activity, right before a trip to Italy with Paul.

I know how to eliminate buckets that aren't serving me, because I've done it before. In the past, I've turned down multi-million-dollar opportunities because they were not right for what was going on in my life at that moment. I didn't see a place for those deals in my realm. When the *Housewives* was no longer enjoyable, when it wasn't where I wanted to be, I stopped it, not once, but twice. Both times, doing the show was affecting other areas of my life, and I didn't feel good about myself. It's not who I was or wanted to be. During the pandemic, I had gotten rid of many personal belongings because they weren't serving me, and I learned that I'd rather have a few good things that I love instead of many that didn't matter to me. It's the same thing with work. I'd rather be doing fewer things that were interesting and meaningful than many things that don't speak to the evolution of my brands or me.

B SMART

Sleep It Off

Consistent, deep sleep is important for our emotional well-being, brain power, immune system, and overall health. Solid, deep, satisfying rest time is good medicine for keeping centered when you're building, flying, jumping, succeeding. A well-rested person is a focused person. I know from past experience, especially as a young woman when I was running around Manhattan getting four hours of sleep a night, that lack of sleep can fuel many negatives. Raw nerves, fuzzy thinking, and a tendency to indulge in other unhealthy behaviors, like eating poorly.

Prioritizing sleep is a discipline. For me, getting in a solid eight hours is particularly beneficial, *especially* when things are going well. Become militant about sleep hygiene. I take sleep so seriously that I use a weighted blanket. I have a Tempur-Pedic pillow that is supportive and helps establish a comfortable resting position. I also try to go to bed at around the same time every night, usually right after I take a hot bath with Epsom salts and sometimes lavender.

If I can, I might do some conscious breathing or meditation or listen to a sleep story using a sleep app on my phone (there are dozens of free sleep apps to choose from). An hour-long walk on the beach, yoga, or any kind of gentle exertion helps me wind down. Even though I try to be strict about a sleep ritual, I also try not to activate myself by worrying about the clock and counting the hours on the rare occasion when I do have trouble falling asleep. I try not to focus too much on what is happening on the following day; it's a good way to avoid nervous energy in the evening. There is one rule I have about sleep that everyone around me knows: don't wake me up. Not for Brad Pitt or Oprah or Queen Elizabeth. Not for anything or anyone. Here is a sleep cheat sheet (no pun intended!) that we should all aspire to. Do the best you can. Sweet dreams.

1. **Make your room dark and your bed comfortable.** Light confuses your body clock, making you think it's daytime. Turn off the lights, install room darkening shades or curtains, and envelop yourself in the dark. Make sure your mattress is comfortable, your sheets soft, and your pillow supportive.

2. **Put the phone down. I don't always put my phone away at night, but I try.** Sure, you can keep the phone on and in your nightstand for emergency purposes, but don't scroll social media, email, or the news before hitting the sack. This stuff keeps your mind agitated. Do the best you can.

3. **Let it wait.** Don't start complex or emotional conversations close to bedtime. Don't think too much about work or get involved in a project. The thinking required will definitely keep you up later than you should be.

4. **Make a note.** If you do have things on your mind, one of the best ways to get them off your mind is to transfer them to paper. Think about keeping a notepad next to the bed so you can quickly jot down ideas or concerns. No need to put pressure on yourself to journal every night—for many people that can create its own kind of anxiety. A dear diary sentence or two can inspire some great ideas...that you can address tomorrow!

5. **Look for help.** I sometimes try melatonin, which is a natural sleep aid, and I use sleep apps on my phone. I try not to have any alcohol before bed, but instead have water. But if it is very late and I need to get to sleep, I choose a few sips of wine instead of staying up all night.

Cut It Out

At some point you need to think about what's causing you to lose track of the buckets, why there may be so many vying for your attention, and whether you are able to give any of them the care they need. It's hard not to feel slightly guilty about cutting back if you take your obligations seriously, as I do. In my case, I have contracts; many people are counting on me to show up. But can these obligations be tended to properly if there are too many of them?

I've talked to many people about this. Some of the tendency to take too much on comes from enthusiasm, which is a nice quality, but it can prevent us from paying attention to the line forming out the door. Some of it is in our nature, which means we have to work a little harder to fix it or come to terms with it, and turn any natural tendencies in our favor, so we can use them to our advantage. Almost anything can become a plus. When I talked about this with English rock superstar Rick Springfield, he said his longtime depression has been difficult for him, and that can often lead to a pile-up of unnecessary demands. It's also what fuels him to make better music, and to want to give his best to his audience.

As for my perfectionism, my incredible attention to details, it has made me the best at producing events, paying strict attention to achieving the best bottom line. My events are seamless, and I see all the facets of the gem. This is the part of me that allows me to see things in business, and in that sense, being in the weeds can be an asset because I read the fine print and think about what it means. My perfectionism allowed me to use all the tools in this book to stay five steps ahead, to see how a contract could have an impact on my future, which led to important clauses and negotiations that foresaw spin-offs from TV shows, or allowed me to do both the *Housewives* and *Shark Tank* at the same time, and to have other businesses without having to give the show a cut. Always look at the big picture and the long journey. You also have to take the rose with the thorns.

> I believe in coming from a place of yes, but that doesn't mean saying yes to everything that rolls your way.

The part of me that sees the little details in business is my super power, but it can also create situations where I can let too many demands into my realm. I don't forget about anything, whether that be a loophole in a contract or a small problem that can turn into a big one, like the swimwear debacle and convincing the HSN models to tell the truth about how they felt about the suits. All of these granular details explain why I'm successful. I'm not successful because I sell jeans or pizza or coffee syrups. I'm successful because of *how* I sell them—and how the deals to make and market them are structured. It's because I think about the fact that the pizza needs to be a little larger for the customer to see the value in its price. The jeans have to be cut a certain way so they flatter a variety of figures, because every woman deserves to look terrific and feel confident in her denim. I am meticulous about how my sunglasses need to feel, and how their cases and polishing cloths need to be made, so they look and feel like true luxury items.

There are many people who are far better known than I am and are far wealthier who have put their names on products just to make money. That is something I have never done and will never do. That means I need an authentic reason to create a new product, and that product has to tell a relevant story that customers relate to. I have had products fail or be short-lived, but none of them have been because they were "smash-and-grab" attempts at simply making money. Everything has had practical reasoning behind it.

Ask yourself why you are saying yes to so many things, and answer the question honestly. I believe in coming from a place of yes, but that doesn't mean saying yes to everything that rolls your way. I talked to actor and author Matthew McConaughey about this. His book *Greenlights* had a powerful impact on me. In it, he talks about coming to a realization that he was selling out his career and not being true to himself.

This powerful realization came to him when he was offered another romantic comedy script, after successfully appearing in similar box office hits. These movies, known in the industry as "rom-coms," were turning into his half-full buckets. He had to find a way to claw his way out of that.

Matthew wanted to transition to more dramatic roles, but no one was interested in him as that kind of leading man. So he left Hollywood and moved to Texas with his family. Soon after, his manager sent him a new rom-com script with an offer of $5 million attached. He said no. Then the producers came back with $8 million, but he didn't think the script was good. He turned it down again. Next, they offered $12 million. No. They came back with a $14.5 million offer. Is the fourth time a charm?

"Now, there was a little lightning bolt. I read the same script one more time, and guess what? It was the exact same words but it was a better script. It was more dramatic, it was funnier. More romantic." He was being sarcastic but also honest about how money can change how we view things and maybe tempt us away from the path we want to go down.

Ultimately, though, he said no one more time. That's when it started to become courageous. There are not many people who could walk away at that point.

What happened next was amazing. "They realized that 'he ain't bluffing,'" he told me. "He's really not doing that. Okay.

Amazing." Matthew had made his point. He was serious about not doing any more rom-coms. "Now, nothing comes in for one year and two months. Then fourteen months…nothing. Now, I think I may have had it in Hollywood. I have to start thinking about new careers. Maybe I want to become a high school football coach, or an orchestra conductor, because I may not ever work in Hollywood again."

After twenty months the phone rang at the McConaughey house. Guess who's now become a new, novel, interesting casting idea for a drama? "During those twenty months of not working was time spent un-branding myself as a rom-com leading man," he explains. Was it nerve-wracking at times? You bet it was. "I was forgotten. People may have thought, 'he's not in our theaters, he's not shirtless on the beach.' Well, there are no beaches in Texas in Austin."

The script he was sent was *The Lincoln Lawyer*, released in 2011 to good reviews. It is a thriller about a lawyer who operates out of his Lincoln, defending a variety of bottom feeders. No surprise Matthew has been the face of Lincoln since 2012. After that movie, McConaughey was offered other dramatic roles, including in *Bernie*, *Magic Mike*, the *Wolf of Wall Street*, and *Killer Joe*. They were all made and released within a two-year span.

Pulling back was worth it. It's a reminder for all of us. It goes right back to what Lorne Michaels said about having to make an exit to make an entrance. I walked away from the *Housewives* and had the courage to stay away for years, walking away from a great deal of money in the process, only to get invited back for more money, and for a lot more power and leverage. I walked away again. My next entrance will be completely different.

Maybe we all cannot turn down work for twenty months; that is probably unrealistic for most of us. However, I believe all of us can hold out for the buckets we want. Maybe that means staying in a job that is not ideal for a couple of months until the right new position opens up. It could be making a few more sacrifices while we give ourselves more time to plan for a change. We can't allow ourselves to get so far gone that we have a meltdown over bed linens. If you do, *you* have to let yourself heal. Shut it down and shut it off. Take a walk. Meditate. Sleep! You also have to play. Take a bath. Breathe. Laugh. All the mottos on those corny decorative signs in gift shops? *They're all true.*

One thing I have discovered is that the best ideas come during those low-energy-expenditure relaxation points. When I'm between sleep and waking, that's when the perfect name for a product comes to me. Problems get solved; revelations arrive. Light bulbs turn on. I can come into a thought from another side.

The break I took after that breakdown was just for a few days. What a difference it made. It was a chance for me to get my head together, rest, meditate, walk, eat well, and then brush myself off and start over fresher and more rested. I was able to come at the challenges and issues I was facing from a different angle and with renewed energy. I have always practiced this strategy, even though sometimes I wait too long, until I crack.

Rest time is about quality versus quantity. Spend time with your children and be present; spend time with your family and your partners and be centered. Likewise, when you're working, be in the moment. You can't give yourself to anything or anyone if there's no more left to give. Don't underestimate the value of laughter.

Now I'm trying to figure out how to stop the ride. I don't want or need any more fame. I don't like wearing makeup; I don't like getting my hair done. I want to be me!

Here are the buckets I want full: Time with my daughter. Room for relaxation. The ability to make time for yoga. The space for good business ideas to come, and then execute them well. More time devoted to raising more money for the B Strong Initiative and expanding that initiative, so that I can have an impact where help is needed the most all around the world. Right now I am expanding to help the homeless and battered women. My podcast. Writing books. Expressing myself creatively.

When I look around at people with tremendous fame, entertainers and actresses, who love to get dressed up, and love fashion and attending all the major social events, such as the Met Ball and the Academy Awards, I see that level of social engagement as a fulltime job. And it is. There are people who thrive on that job; those are their buckets. Ironically, those buckets never get filled because no one can be the prettiest, the richest, and so on. They aren't my buckets. I like being free, unshackled, and untethered. I like to have the time to be with my daughter, relax with a friend and sip a margarita, and not care about looking good but instead focus on being healthy and strong. That's what makes me happy.

EPILOGUE

What Makes You Happy?

IF YOU WANT TO BE SUCCESSFUL IN BUSINESS, YOU HAVE ALL THE tools you need to help you get there in this book. Pick what you want from the ingredients I have given you and create your own recipe. The most important lesson to take away as you create your personal alchemy of tips and strategies is that while you're striving, stop every once in a while and check in with yourself to make sure you are *thriving* as well. Invest in yourself! It's the very best investment you can make.

Never forget to live your life in the present. Enjoy your experiences, and learn from the ups and downs. Savor the moments that make you the most happy. Appreciate your mistakes for what they teach you.

You don't need to have all the answers right now. Let them reveal themselves as you work your way toward your goals.

Don't confine yourself to certain fixed ideas, or be overly concerned about what other people think you should do or want you to do. Don't allow yourself to be shackled to one version of life and therefore miss all the things that your life could be instead.

Set yourself up for success by understanding what gives you the best return on investment in your life, including business, friendships, charitable work, creating memories and experiences, making time for celebrations from New Year's to Fourth of July, Halloween, Thanksgiving, Chanukah and Christmas, birthdays to just a regular Friday night, a sunny Saturday, or a rainy Sunday afternoon. All of it. Those moments when you take the time to honor the day and the fact that you're here, those are the times that people remember. Traditions, snuggles, tailgating, Sunday pasta—that's what matters. Business, life, love, family, and charity all have one thing in common: what you put into them comes out and back to you. What habits make you feel healthiest, strongest, and ready to face the challenges of entrepreneurship? Remember, business *is* personal! I get a big return from spending time with my daughter. That's a bucket that I want to overflow.

Maybe you operate better on one glass of wine at the end of the day instead of two or three. Maybe water in between two glasses of wine makes sense for you. Maybe you operate better on less sugar and more exercise, or more sleep and less sex, or maybe you want to give up a little sleep to have more sex. Maybe you do better when you can stretch and practice yoga than you do trying to do serious workouts at the gym. Does eating mostly plants make you feel better, or do you need protein to be kick-ass?

You will be moody, you will want to get off the ride, at times your partner will seem unattractive and irritating, your kids will drive you crazy one day and the next day they will make you cry with joy. Strive for balance, even if it seems impossible. Keep going.

Most of all, be good to yourself. Take chances even when you're afraid of the unknown. Get on the road; move forward, improve yourself, learn something new every day, work hard but stop and smell the roses.

ACKNOWLEDGMENTS

Thank you to Karen Kelly. I know my process is unique and crazy and immersive. You trusted my nontraditional way of attacking a book like this, and I'm truly proud of what we have accomplished. This was a crazy time in the world and this circuitous writing journey is reflective of that.

Thanks to Andy McNicol. You have in many ways been a pandemic cliché. Weathering a serious hit during that unprecedented time, you rose from the ashes like so many strong women this book is written for. We sprang into action and made this important piece of work come to light. I look forward to more projects together. You are proof that corporations are made of the people in their offices versus the names on the side of the building.

Thanks to everyone at Hachette who helped make this book a reality: my editor Lauren Marino, publisher Mary Ann Naples, Michelle Aielli, associate publisher, Michael Barrs, head of marketing, Michael Giarratano, my publicist, Julianne Lewis, my marketer, Rebecca Maines for her copyediting skills, and Amanda Kain for the amazing photo shoot and cover design. You gave me

independence and autonomy, and allowed me to be me, and tell my story in my way. There is no greater gift you can give to a writer.

This has been the most enjoyable, seamless professional journey and experience working with a publisher to date. It's been a crazy and unprecedented time in our world and we all kept our heads down and had faith in the processes as if the world wasn't upside down. There has been a balanced energy surrounding this project, which I infinitely appreciate. We each did our part, and the final product is incredible. We are teed up for greatness. You are superb in your approach and process. Thank you for that.

Thank you Bryn, my peanut. You are the love and light of my life. So much of my love for you and experiences as your mother has guided me. I have learned everything out of wanting to be strong for you, and to make you proud. I want you to chart your own course and be your own girl and woman—your happiness is paramount, your love drives me, and your sweet and creative spirit makes you my true north. I love you more than anything and hope this book drives you to do and be anything you set your mind to in this life and world.

Thank you to Paul for being such a solid, strong, and loving partner. Your support is endless, and your love is infinite. I appreciate you listening to and consulting on my endless business and personal struggles and triumphs. I love you.